Africa since Independence

Africa
since
Independence

Colin Legum

INDIANA UNIVERSITY PRESS
BLOOMINGTON AND INDIANAPOLIS

THIS BOOK IS A PUBLICATION OF

INDIANA UNIVERSITY PRESS

601 NORTH MORTON STREET

BLOOMINGTON IN 47404-3797 USA

HTTP://WWW.INDIANA.EDU/~IUPRESS

TELEPHONE ORDERS 800-842-6796

FAX ORDERS 812-855-7931

ORDERS BY E-MAIL IUPORDER@INDIANA.EDU

© 1999 BY COLIN LEGUM

THE PAPER USED IN THIS PUBLICATION MEETS THE MINIMUM REQUIREMENTS OF AMERICAN NATIONAL STANDARD FOR INFORMATION SCIENCES—PERMANENCE OF PAPER FOR PRINTED LIBRARY MATERIALS, ANSI Z39.48-1984.

MANUFACTURED IN THE UNITED STATES OF AMERICA.

LIBRARY OF CONGRESS CATALOGING-IN-PUBLICATION DATA

LEGUM, COLIN

AFRICA SINCE INDEPENDENCE / COLIN LEGUM

    P.   CM.

INCLUDES INDEX.

ISBN 0-253-33588-4 (ALK. PAPER).—ISBN 0-254-21334-7 (PBK. : ALK. PAPER)

    1. AFRICA—POLITICS AND GOVERNMENT—1960-I. TITLE

DT30.5.L44 1999

960.3'2—DC21   99-29505

1 2 3 4 5 04 03 02 01 00 99

For my wife Margaret

My sternest and most valued critic

Contents

Acknowledgments

This book had its origins in a series of lectures I was privileged to give in 1997 as a Distinguished Fellow of the Institute for Advanced Studies at Indiana University in Bloomington.

My wife and I are grateful to Dave and Ruth Albright for their help in organizing our Fellowships, and to the Institute's remarkable director, Henry Remak.

February 1988

KOB Cottage
Kalk Bay
Cape Peninsula 7975
South Africa

Africa since Independence

The Romantic Period, 1939-1970

Oh sons and daughters of Africa,
Flesh of the sun, and flesh of the sky,
Let us make Africa the tree of life.
Let all of us unite and toil together
To give the best we have to Africa
The cradle of mankind and fount of culture.
Pride and hope at break of dawn
—Last two verses of the Anthem of the
Organization of African Unity

Africa has passed through three phases in its learning cycle since independence: the innocence of inexperience and the euphoria of the early romantic period; the disillusioning experience of adolescents (in this case, young nations) growing up in an adverse environment; and, finally, coming to terms with reality.

The modern period of African romanticism covered roughly a quarter of a century from the end of World War II to the early 1970s. In the West, no less than in Africa, it was a time of optimism and high hopes for the renaissance of a continent.

At the end of the war, there were only four independent

states in the continent—Egypt, Ethiopia, Liberia, and South Africa; over the next fifteen years the number almost quadrupled, but the hardest part of the decolonization process still lay ahead—in Algeria, South West Africa, Rhodesia, the Portugese colonies, and South Africa. Even though romanticism began to lose some of its optimistic innocence after the mid-1960s, confidence was still growing in the freshly sovereign states that their demand of "Africa for Africans" was irresistible. Economic growth, averaging between 6 and 8 percent, promised a brighter future.

What is the Africa we are talking about? Is it the Africa seen through Western eyes—a huge underdeveloped land mass that is home to 650 million people (11 percent of the world's population); a continent which has slid into economic ruin, corruption, despotic rule, coups, and civil wars? Or is it a continent seen through African eyes? If so, which African eyes? To read about Africa as described by African poets and intellectuals is not to read about the condition of one continent, but rather the conditions of many societies at different levels of political, social, and economic development. Allowing for errors arising from generalization, there are broadly speaking only two attitudes about which it can be said there is an African consensus—two refrains which I hear wherever I travel in the continent. The first is that at the core of independence is the assertion of dignity of a Black people which was relentlessly assaulted by colonialism, but never destroyed, not even by the worst form of colonialism—slavery; the second refrain is that the West is to blame for the poverty and fragmented disarray found in Africa. Nevertheless, attitudes to the West are strongly ambivalent, expressing both admiration of Western achievements and hatred of its hypocrisies and Eurocentric selfishness; this ambivalence is matched by Western attitudes and feeling toward Africa and Black people in general. The Indian poet Tagore traced the source of this ambivalence to the civilization of the West—the upholding of dignity and of human relationships had no place in the administration of its colonies. Tagore's explanation was reduced to a brilliant single Shavian sentence by Nehru when asked what he thought of Western civilization. "It would," he replied, "be a good idea."

To understand contemporary attitudes in postcolonial Africa and the West it is useful, indeed necessary, to keep in mind this love–hate relationship between the formerly colonized people and the colonizers; the former believe there has been no proper recognition of, nor retribution for, the injury of colonialism; while the latter feel let down because Africa has not lived up to the expectations of European liberal values; and, of course, Western racial-ists—an ancient and self-perpetuating breed—see all their own prejudices about Black people justified by the selec-tive headlines provided for them by the myopia of a media society which traps them in non-thinking stereotypes such as presenting Africa as "a basket-case continent."

Few writers, in my experience, express more clearly— and more elegantly—an African view of the continent than does K. Anthony Appiah—himself the son of a clever if mercurial Ghanaian politician, and grandson of a former British Chancellor of the Exchequer, Sir Stafford Cripps:

> We are speaking of a continent of hundreds of mil-
> lions of people. We are talking of hundreds of languages.
> A thousand years of Christianity before it was established
> in most of Europe, and before Islam was settled in Egypt.
> African Kingships were millennia old. Africans wor-
> shipped thousands of gods whose posterity remains in
> shrines all over the continent. Long before Charlemagne
> was crowned, the ancestors of San people in Southern
> Africa were living in nomadic communities free of rulers.
> Female regiments in Dahomey (now Benin), matrilineal
> kingdoms in Asanti, and patrilineal kingdoms in Yoruba.
> Religious diversity, political diversity, diversity in cloth-

ing and cuisine—Africa has enough diversity to satisfy the wildest "multiculturist."[1]

Except for the Dahomeyan female regiments and the matrilineal kingdoms of Asanti, this description of a continent rich in cultural diversity survives to this day, and is reflected in the characteristics of political parties and societies peculiar to each of Africa's fifty-three states. To speak of Africa as a single continent is accurate only in geographic terms. In other aspects, Africa is even more diverse than Europe or Asia.

In earlier times, Westerners drew a dividing line between the Islamic states of Morocco, Tunisia, Algeria, Libya, and Egypt, and the largely non-Islamic states of Sub-Saharan Africa. This dividing line between what the French called *Afrique blanc* and *Afrique noire* makes no more political sense than the Mason-Dixon line. There are, today, almost as many Black Muslims living around the southern and eastern perimeter of the Sahara as there are to its north.

Except for four hundred years of Portuguese rule over their few territorial "possessions," and three centuries of Dutch and English rule in the Cape, colonialism had shallow historic roots in the continent. Most colonialism in Africa began just over a century before its end. Long before colonialism, much of Sub-Saharan Africa (SSA) was devastated by the slave trade, first with the Arab states of the Middle East, and later with the colonizers of the New World. (There is a tendency, today, to speak only of the slavery in the New World.) Slavery stretched from the Sudan and Mauritania in the north to the Eastern Congo and Malawi in the south, and along both the Indian Ocean and Atlantic coasts. In his *Biography of the Continent* (Knopf 1999), the historian John Reader calculates that without the slave trade, Africa's population might have been anything from 40 to 100 percent larger in 1850 than the actual figure of 50–60 million. I know of no adequate study into the effects of the slave trade on African minds and society. Even today it remains embedded in the African psyche, sometimes expressed as anti-European or anti-Arab attitudes and feelings, and sometimes in what Jung called the "ethnic memory."

In the early 1960s, when on a visit to Maiduguri, I visited a small tribe who lived high up in Gwoza on the Cameroon mountains. Only in daylight did members of the tribe venture to the plains below to fetch water, feeling truly safe only in their mountain villages where, more than a century earlier, they had taken refuge from slavers.

In the late 1950s, serious rioting broke out in Blantyre (Malawi) over the arrival in the stores of a new consignment of a brand of corned beef with a picture of a red hand on the label. The locals claimed the corned beef was made from African hands cut off by the slavers.

One night in the mid-1960s I returned late to my hotel in Lagos from a trip to Benin. I was passing luggage out of my car to a porter when he suddenly dropped one of the carvings I had bought and ran screaming in terror into the night. The carving was of a slave, bound and gagged as if for transport. The young porter, who came from a notorious slave-collecting area in Warri, had an imprint of slaving so strong, even centuries later, that he was terrified by even a carved representation of a slave.

Although the war against the colonial invaders never stopped, it was not until the Second World War that the modern anticolonial struggle spread from Indonesia and Indochina in the East across Southeast Asia, the Middle East, and Africa to the Caribbean. Two principal factors account for the decline of western imperialism. World War II had depleted the military and economic resources of the metropolitan powers; the propaganda of a war "fought for democracy" infected public opinion and governments in Europe, as well as anti-imperialist movements in the colo-

THE ROMANTIC PERIOD, 1939–1970

nies led by modernizing elites. The other factor was that colonial possessions had begun to lose their economic value for Britain and France, though not yet for Portugal, Spain, and Belguim. The British socialist economist John Strachey wrote an impressive study of this latter factor in *The End of Empire.*[2] There were, of course, other contributing factors, such as American pressure on the colonial powers, especially on the Dutch in Indonesia; the inspiration of a non-white power like Japan confronting the Western powers; and the "spectre" of the USSR spreading its anti-Western influence in the postwar world. Political analysts differ in their assessments of the weight to be assigned to each of these factors, but few doubt that the major factors were the commitment to a postwar democratic world order, and that the colonies had lost or were losing their economic value and had become, or were becoming, an increasing burden. By the end of the war, the African anti-colonial movements were swept along on the incoming tide of promised freedom for all, though what this meant was by no means clear.

The situation in the immediate postwar years was that Egypt had shaken off the British yoke, the United Nations had ended Libya's trusteeship, Emperor Haile Selassie was back on his throne in Ethiopia, Liberia remained the solitary independent state in West Africa, and South Africa had embarked in 1948 on its disastrous course as an apartheid state. France and Britain had begun to walk different paths in an effort to slow down the advance to full independence. The French, under the Bonapartiste de Gaulle, proposed a form of autonomy and federalism in West and Central Africa; the British yielded under the pressure of a threatening violent situation to grant independence to the Gold Coast. The birth of Ghana on 6 March 1957 was to prove to be as significant an event for the African continent as the independence of India had been for Asia just ten years earlier. Within seven years, all of British and Francophone Africa south of the Sahara and north of the Zambezi had sloughed off its colonial status. Thus, in Africa, the domino theory proved to be correct.

Two remarkable factors about the decolonization of the vast African continent were the speed with which it occurred and the relative absence of violence. Except for three countries—Sudan, where a civil war with largely religious roots broke out on the morning after independence; Algeria, where a prolonged and bitter war began; and Rwanda, where the Hutu asserted their majority claim to rule over the Tutsis in the small new republic, thereby unleashing an ethnic conflict that still persists. In addition to Algeria, the worst violence occurred in those countries with significant populations of White settlers—South Africa, Rhodesia, and Kenya—and in Angola, Mozambique, and the Congo, where two metropolitan powers—Portugal and Belgium—sought to resist the flow of history.

The uneasy years between the end of World War Two and the independence of Ghana were a time of the dispersal of new ideas and the emergence of several distinctive types of African leaders—conservatives and left-wing militant radicals. These two developments influenced both the direction of the anticolonial struggle and the different types of postcolonial regimes.

Among the influential conservatives were King Hassan of Morocco, President Tubman of Liberia, Emperor Haile Selassie of Ethiopia, Philibert Tsiranana of Madagascar, Leopold Senghor of Senegal, Jomo Kenyatta of Kenya (who began as a radical but ended up as a conservative), Felix Houphouet-Boigny of Côte d'Ivoire, Kamazu (Hastings) Banda of Malawi, Seretse Khama of Botswana, and Abubakr Tafawa Balewa of Nigeria.

When my wife and I interviewed Houphouet-Boigny in Abidjan in 1960, he told us: "I am not prepared to call for my country's independence because we are not ready for it. Only when our people can compete on equal terms with the French will we be justified in taking our independence—and that might only come in the lifetime of my grandson!" These were the sentiments of a French doctor and a former leader of the radical Rassemblement Democratique Africaine (RDA) which, in the war years, had worked with the French Communist Party. Yet, within two years of that interview, Houphouet-Boigny was forced for his own survival to lead his country into independence.

Against the conservatives were ranged two camps of radicals and militants. Though close to each other, they did not agree upon either tactics or goals. The radicals— like the joint father of Nigerian nationalism, Dr. Nnamdi Azikiwe (known as Zik), Julius Nyerere of Tanzania, Tom Mboya of Kenya, Habib Bourguiba of Tunisia, Milton Obote of Uganda, Kenneth Kaunda of Zambia, and Eduardo Mondlane of Mozambique—were pragmatists, reformers, and non-Marxists wary of Moscow. The militants— who included Kwame Nkrumah of Ghana, General Nasser of Egypt, Samora Machel of Mozambique, Sékou Touré of Guinea, Modiba Keita of Mali, Ben Balla of Algeria, Robert Mugabe of Zimbabwe, and Amilcar Cabral of Guinea-Bissau—were a mixture of revolutionaries and supporters of violent movements; they were strong proponents of Pan-Africanism and (except for Ben Bella) were influenced by Marxist ideas.

These are crude classifications which do not take into account, for example, King Hassan's decision to join the militant Casablanca Group of Pan-Africanists against the Monrovia Group led by Liberia and Nigeria; or Julius Nyerere, who was a militant agrarian reformer and a passionate Pan-Africanist opposed to the speed and methods urged by Nkrumah, a devout Catholic and egalitarian socialist and critic of Marxism. Others, like Patrice Lumumba and Nelson Mandela, began as radicals and ended up as reformers because of their experiences in the struggle. There were also rapid shifts in the positions of leaders depending on their perceptions of immediate interests. Consider the case of Joshua Nkomo of Zimbabwe. He was a "bourgeois" nationalist who, because he was losing out in the power struggle with Mugabe (who had fallen under the spell of Mao Tse-tung), took himself off to Moscow, which was always keen to support any opponent of what it chose to classify as a pro-Chinese leader; Nkomo was welcomed despite his anti-communist credentials and his close ties with Tiny Rowland of Lonrho in the city of London.

The advent in the 1960s of the USSR and China on the African continent—first as allies and then as bitter rivals—provided opportunities for African leaders to play the Communist powers off against each other and both against the West, as well as pitting Bonn and Paris against London and Washington. The ultra-conservative Muslim Siad Barre of Somalia overnight declared his country a Marxist state in alliance with Moscow, because the Western powers were supporting Somalia's enemy, Haile Selassie; but when Moscow switched its support to the Emperor's successor, Mengistu Haile Mariam, Barre swung sharply against Moscow and toward Washington. Except for Mengistu, no African leader or regime was ever a serious or reliable Communist ally. They were "rhetorical" Marxists adept at using Marxist slogans but loath to erect communist institutions; for example, a professed Marxist regime in the Congo People's Republic always relied on budget support from France. At the height of the Cold War, when Africans were loosening, though very few were breaking, their ties with the West, the hawks in Washington and in some European capitols became paranoid about the possibility of Africa being "lost" to the West. They did not believe the martyred Tom Mboya when he declared that the postindependence African leaders were "neither pro-Moscow nor pro-West, they are pro-African." This was a simple idea but was apparently very difficult for the major western powers to grasp, seeing the Soviet interest in the postcolonial world as a potential threat to their strategic interests, while the Soviets saw African left-wingers as possible allies to their anti-Western cause.

The high-stakes three-handed diplomatic game played during the years of the Cold War had unfortunate consequences for independent Africa, highlighted by such events as the Suez crisis; the Cuban-Soviet-US confrontation; the South African role in fuelling the war in Angola; the murder of Lumumba; and the overthrow of Nkrumah.

These fugitive thoughts about the Cold War, Western postcolonial policies, and the place of communism in the liberation struggles are a good moment to turn to the spread of new political ideas in the time leading up to African emancipation.

Unlike the Indian experience with the emergence of a pro-Japanese "national army," African sympathies during World War II were fully with the Allies, because a German victory was seen as bringing in a new period of imperialism by the Nazis with their Aryan race theories, whereas an Allied victory held out the promise of the end of imperialism. The belief that emancipation awaited only a final Allied victory bred confidence; by the end of the war the only serious question being debated was the political shape of postimperial Africa—capitalist and pro-West, said the conservatives; socialist and non-aligned, said the radicals and militants.

The last major resistance to the imperial conquest in the nineteenth and early twentieth centuries had been led by traditionalists whose base was in the rural areas—in the Rift Valley of Morocco, the forests of Guinea, Zululand in Natal, the Asanti Confederacy in the Gold Coast, the Hereros in South West Africa, and the Wahehe of Tanganyika. All failed. The new African leadership was an almost entirely Western-educated modernizing elite. They were leaders who could fight their colonizers in their own language, using their political weapons, and challenging them on their own liberal democratic principles.

Their ideas for governing Africa were also derived from the West—separation of powers between the executive, legislative, and administrative institutions; *habeas corpus;* an independent judiciary; respect for the rights of minorities; press freedom; a non-political professional army; independent trade unions; and other ideals. Few questioned the virtues and values of an idealized Western democracy. The only difference, the new African leaders argued, "is that unlike colonialists we will run our institutions democratically and, so, better and more efficiently." Few questioned the practicability of establishing these age-old institutions in new evolving states or their relevance to the building of new nation-states in countries where, unlike the examples in the history of Europe, the state was established before the nation was properly formed. Reading the speeches and writings of the modernizing African elites from the 1940s to the 1960s, one is struck by two major facts: enthusiasm for a multi-party democracy and confidence about the kind of institutions needed to replace the centralized colonial state maintained by the baton and the gun. Nowhere have I found in African writing—or for that matter in the studies by Western writers—expression of the possibility that Africa's postcolonial history would be written so largely by soldiers. There were those like Julius Nyrerere, who, before Tanganyika's independence, echoed Nehru's view: "We don't need an army after independence."

Throughout the continent, with the solitary exception of Swaziland, the inheritors of the power to rule were local modernizing elites. Most of them were urbanized and had at least some secondary education. In West Africa, especially, they included the sons and daughters of traditional leaders and so provided a link between the capitol and the countryside. Some leaders combined their traditional role

THE ROMANTIC PERIOD, 1939-1970

with their role in the modernizing elite system—such as Houphouet-Boigny, who spent much of his political life in Paris and Abidjan, but retained his roots in his native Baule country. This duality was true also of Seretse Khama and his formidable uncle, Tshekedi, the maker of Botswana's independence; and of the Zulu chief Albert Luthuli, who led the African National Congress through a difficult period. (Although Nelson Mandela comes from a royal family, he played no role in Tembu [a major Xhosa clan] traditional affairs.)

Traditional Africa remained very much alive at the coming of independence, but it was marginalized by the modernizing elites. In the same way that life in the rural countryside was undermined by the Industrial Revolution so, too, the priority given by the new political class to the modern sector in Africa resulted in the cities becoming powerful magnets for the impoverished, unemployed rural dwellers.

The modernizing elites comprised only a tiny percentage of each country's population. They owed their power to three principal factors: education; a dominant role in the professions, commerce, and the civil service; and, above all, the fact that the population widely accepted them as the only people qualified to take over the colonial state and capable of delivering on the promise of a better life.

The anticolonial struggle triggered what came to be known as "a revolution of rising expectations," and fuelled African nationalism throughout the continent. Led by modernizing elites, this nationalist fervor inspired mass movements which, at a later stage, were converted into competing political parties. (I use elites in a plural form because there were several competing elite groups with different traditions and backgrounds.) The surprising phenomenon was the similarity of their political ideas, even though they had passed through different educational systems—Protestant and Catholic mission schools; Islamic centers; British private and public schools; the French bac-

calaureate; European, American, and South African univer-
sities and colleges; and later also Russian and other Eastern
European higher education institutions. Even though those
coming from Anglophone or Francophone countries had
rarely met each other before independence and most were
unable to read what was written in each other's language,
their political ideas were little different. This was perhaps
not surprising, since their ideas were eclectically chosen
from Western constitutions, political and social concepts,
principles, and practices. For example, the concept of the
nation-state was appropriated wholesale.

In his book *The Black Man's Burden,* historian Basil
Davidson blames the failure of postindependence Africa on
the uncritical adoption of the nation-state at independence. But what other choice did African leaders have?
Responding to Davidson, another historian, Joseph Ki-
Zerbo of Burkina Faso, agreed that "the nation-state has
become Africa's principal burden," but he asked: If we
renounce the nation-state where do we go?[3] Davidson's
answer is "to federalism"; Ki-Zerbo's reply is that federalism, *vide* Nigeria, does not necessarily undo the internal
contradictions in embryonic nation-states.

This kind of debate found little place in the pre-independence discussions among the makers of modern Africa.
Except in the case of Nigeria, federalism was seen as a
threat to the creation of a unified, multiethnic state, as
well as likely to strengthen secessionist movements. These
were the reasons, for example, why, in the lengthy negotiations over South Africa's new democratic constitution, the
ANC strongly fought against the idea of federalism; it
remains the "f-word" in the ANC's political lexicon. On
the other hand, despite the threatened breakaway of the
Ibo-led Biafra state, federalism remains entrenched in
Nigeria, and was accepted as the basis for Ethiopia's first
democratic constitution.

The sharpest difference between the evolution of the

nation-state in Western Europe and in Sub-Saharan Africa (SSA) was that, in the European experience, the modern state grew out of the formation of nations, whereas in Africa the boundaries and machinery of the state were created by the colonial powers before the nation was formed. Thus the historic power of forming nation-states was stood on its head in SSA. Except for three smaller states—Swaziland, Bechuanaland (Botswana), and Basutoland (Lesotho)—none of the other countries had culturally homogeneous societies. A country like Tanganyika had one hundred and fifty-six ethnic communities (tribes). Nigeria had three national groups and one sub-national group, in addition to some eighty minority groups.

Nation-building was obviously the top priority for the new independent states; but before they achieved power, the anticolonial leaders angrily dismissed the fears of those who predicted that "tribalism" posed a great threat to the stability of the new states: they argued, with heat and conviction, that the defeat of colonialism would put an end to the divide-and-rule policies of imperialists and would facilitate the process of creating a single nationhood.

In the same way that the anticolonial movements unquestioningly took over the idea of the nation-state, all but one, Swaziland, mostly took over the institutions of government established by the colonial regimes. The only immediate difference was that black faces replaced white faces in civil service, the ministries, the judiciary, and, after a few years, also the top positions in the army and the police. In the early years of independence, no radical institutional reforms were made: where the occupants of key civil service positions under the inherited system clashed with the policies of the new ministers and ruling party officials, they were forced to either accept orders or face dismissal. In this way, while the previous framework of colonial institutions was retained, the practice became distorted. Instead of a system which ostensibly sought to maintain checks and balances, authority rapidly shifted to a ruling party dominated by an executive presidency and a centralized bureaucratic form of government.

Another major weakness at the time of independence was the lack of trained administrators and technicians. When Zambia became independent in 1964, it had only one hundred and nine African college graduates, none of whom had administrative experience at a senior level. The situation was even worse in the Congo (Zaire, now Congo Democratic Republic), where there were only sixteen college graduates at independence, none of whom had held a senior position. Although Northern Rhodesia (Zambia) had a major mining industry, there was not a single African qualified in metallurgy or other mining techniques.[4]

The situation was somewhat better in West Africa, which boasted some outstanding administrators—Robert Gardiner, Daniel Chapman, and Yao Adu in Gold Coast (Ghana); Ivor Cummings in Sierra Leone; and Simeon Adebo in Nigeria. Men like these came into early conflict with the new political class over three principal issues: insistence on maintaining a properly defined relationship between civil servants and ministers; the speed of Africanization embarked upon as a natural wish by the new regimes to "decolonize" the administration; and, especially, over qualifications of new senior appointees; and early incidents of nepotism and corruption.

How much did Marxism influence the thinking of the new political class? To answer this question, it is necessary to revert to the earlier reference to the division among the pre-independence leaders as conservatives, reformers, radicals, and militants. It is not too difficult to see why, since fighting colonialism involved fighting the Western colonial powers, most militants and some radicals should have adopted pro-Soviet positions or favored alliances with communist parties. Even Felix Houphouet-Boigny allied himself with French communist movements in the Second

World War years. Moreover, since colonialism was seen as "capitalist imperialism" it was not surprising that some of its challengers should have sought a possible alternative in what Arnold Toynbee described as "a Western heresy," Marxism.

Left-wing African nationalists seldom distinguished between Marxist socialism, i.e. communism, and democratic socialism. Their heresy in the eyes of the Comintern and its successor, the Cominform, was to invent the concept of "African socialism." As in Asia, where Jesuits argued that Christianity could best be proselytized by adopting a "local dress," so in Africa Marxism was revised by some to meet local conditions. An archmilitant, Sékou Touré of Guinea, explained the need for this: "The Marxism which served to mobilize the African populations and in particular, the working class, and to lead that class to success, has been amputated of those of its characteristics which did not correspond to the African realities." Expressing a somewhat different view, Kwame Nkrumah of Ghana said the aims of the Convention People's Party (the CPP) "embrace the creation of a welfare state based upon Ghanaian conditions in which all citizens, regardless of class, tribe, color or creed, shall have equal opportunity. Our party also seeks to promote popular democracy based upon universal suffrage — on the basis of one man, one vote." Most left-wing Africans, like Sékou Touré and Nkrumah, rejected the class struggle as being irrelevant to Africa because they argued there were no class divisions like those of Europe in the African continent.

Because the colonial economy was almost exclusively in the hands of foreign businesses, trading companies, and banks, almost all postindependence governments, conservative or radical, established parastatal companies to gain control over the private sector either through nationalization or through regulation. One outcome was a plethora of parastatals.

Parliamentary democracy is an elastic concept, as the different systems in Europe and the Americas illustrate. During the period under present discussion, serious doubts had not yet surfaced about the value or essential characteristics of a parliamentary government. The anticolonial elites disagreed among themselves, not about the applicability of parliamentary democracy to Africa, but over such issues as the place of an organized opposition. As might be expected, opposition leaders, like Chief O. O. Awolowo and Nnamde Azikiwe, both of Nigeria, argued that an organized opposition was a prerequisite for a parliamentary democracy, while those who held early office, like the Nigerian prime minister, Sir Abubakr Tafawa Balewa; President Sylvanus Olympio of Togo; President Leopold Senghor of Senegal; and the golden boy of Kenyan politics, Tom Mboya, took the opposite view. At least in the early stages of independence, they argued, a strong organized opposition could be a destabilizing force. Julius Nyerere, whose party had won an honest 97 percent of the vote in Tanganyika's pre-independence elections, gave his influential support to the idea of "consensus politics" and single-party rule, which he claimed was the traditional form of government in Africa—a generalization based on the way pre-modern pastoral societies governed themselves in some parts of the continent. Others, especially in West Africa, cited examples of the institutionalization of opposition in traditional societies—for example, the mechanism for dethroning unpopular chiefs. In Benin, at the same time a new king was crowned, an independent chief was elected with the sole function of reminding the king of his accountability and vulnerability to the popular will.

Two future developments were foreshadowed by events early in the independent period: a tendency toward democratic centralism and the personalization of power. Before the assassination by the military of Togo's first president, Sylvanus Olympio, in 1962, nobody had foreseen the possibility of the military playing a dominant role in government. The development of a democratic centralist state soon turned into a bureaucratic state and non-democratic state. These changes were advocated by leaders such as Nkrumah, Sékou Touré, and Modiba Keita after they began to encounter serious opposition. Keita's description of the basis of democratic centralism was that "the Party and the State are the same; both rest on the 'people's will,' and they must be democratically consulted in the formation of policy."

The idea of the one party state—formally declared and embodied in a constitution—was first taken up and implemented by Nyerere in Tanganyika, because he could claim that the almost 100 percent electoral support won by his ruling party, Tanu, constituted a mandate for a one party state; but he also believed that democratic principles and practices within such a state had to be institutionalized. Nyerere's championing of a one party state triggered a debate on the meaning of democracy in Africa. Nyerere himself confessed: "I have my own doubts about the suitability for Africa of the Anglo-Saxon form of democracy." Thirty years later, he was to change his mind. Among those leading the debate against Nyerere was Leopold Senghor. "If I thought Africans could not produce a democracy," he said, "I would leave politics."

Ethnicity in a continent of more than a thousand tribes was obviously a concern of the new rulers of Africa; but tribalism was a taboo subject: anybody raising questions about tribalism risked being denounced as a racist. The usual line of criticism was that tribalism had been used by colonialists to divide and rule. This was undeniably true. The nationalist approach was to see the only solution to "cultural plurality" was through the creation of supra-tribal loyalties to the evolving new nation, but without destroying local community ties and loyalties. Nation-building, therefore, became a top priority of the embryonic nation-state. However, loyalties and interests were not easily surmountable and were a major source of the post-independence crises that destabilized many of the new states and determined the shape of political parties, as well as the character of their constitutions. This was especially true of countries in which the victorious liberation movements did not involve long-established powerful regimes and strong opposition parties. Such examples included the Brong-Asanti confederacy in Ghana; Awolowo's Yoruba-based Action Group in West Nigeria; and the Buganda Kingdom in Uganda.

One issue that featured prominently in the anticolonial campaign was the arrogant way in which the European powers had carved up Africa at the 1886 Berlin conference, creating artificial boundaries which, in places, divided ethnic communities. In the West, fears were widely expressed that reparative action would be taken after independence to right these wrongs, as had been the South American experience, and that this would produce serious border conflicts. These fears proved to be largely groundless. The few conflicts that did occur were minor affairs—briefly between Algeria and Morocco, between Mali and Niger, and Chad and Libya; there were political tensions rather than violence between Togo and Ghana over the Ewe fault-line, and occasional minor skirmishes between Nigeria and Cameroon. The one serious war, between Ethiopia and Eritrea, was fought not over borders, but over the latter's claim to the sovereignty of which they were deprived by the Italian colonizing power. One reason no wars were fought over borders in Africa was because the post-independence leaders had decided in an act of statesmanship that the boundaries of the new independent states should be those inherited from the colonial powers, and that no rectification brought about by force would be recognized. This stance was entrenched by a decision of the Organization of African Unity (OAU).

Africa came to its independence as a balkanized continent. This condition was historic and not the result of colonialism; on the contrary, the imperialists had reduced the hundreds of territorial entities, emirates, kingdoms, and principalities to fewer than sixty.

Nevertheless, few of the new sovereign states were capable of ever achieving economic viability on their own—a weakness that could be overcome, if at all, only by creating regional and continental economic groupings. This was to become a major priority of the not-yet-born Organization of African Unity. After the completion of the continent's independence, there were fifty-three mainland and island states. More than half of the total population lived in five countries (Nigeria, Egypt, Ethiopia, South Africa, and Zaire). The other half lived in six countries with populations of between fifteen and twenty-four million, four countries with populations of between ten and fifteen million, eighteen countries with populations between five and ten million, ten countries with populations between two and three million, and eight countries with populations between half a million and two million. Moreover, most of these countries—including those with populations the same as that of a large suburb in the United States—cover vast territories. Zaire, for example is the size of all the European countries stretching from Italy, Switzerland, and France through Germany and Holland to Denmark.

The romantic idea of one day uniting the continent into a single political state had its origins not in Africa but among the descendants of African slaves in the New World.[5] Feeling themselves "aliens and exiles," poets and intellectuals dreamed of their Lost Paradise not as a fragmented continent, but as described by African American poet, Langston Hughes, as "one motherland, identity and a sense of oneness between all those Negro Stock whether in Africa or the diaspora." Emphasizing the sense of common identity, he wrote:

> We are related—you and I.
> You from the West Indies.
> I from Kentucky.
> We are related—you and I,
> You from Africa,
> I from the States,
> We are brothers—you and I.

The romantic ideas of the American, West Indian, and French-speaking poets, populist politicians like the Jamaican Marcus Garvey, and intellectuals like W. E. B. Du Bois were carried over into Europe and then into Africa itself by the wartime generation of students and exiles, like Kwame Nkrumah, in America and Britain. This romantic dream of those who "cry among the skyscrapers, as our ancestors cried among the palms in Africa" was inspirational to the movement's leaders who succeeded in creating the Organization of African Unity (OAU) in 1967. Although groups among the Slavs and Latin Americans had struggled to form "Pan" movements in their regions, Africans were the first in history to succeed in doing so. The unique achievement owed its birth to several factors: The psychological feeling that "the Black races"—the oppressed colonial peoples of an entire continent—were indeed "one people" and should demonstrate to the world that this was so; the percieved problems that a balkanized continent held for the newly independent states; the belief that if the continent was to make itself felt both in negotiations with the former colonial powers and in international forums like the United Nations, its best chance of success was to speak, as far as possible, with one voice; the need for an organization to settle boundary and other disputes between the new states, and to pursue the overarching goal of creating machinery for the eventual establishment of a continental economic union based on five economic regions.

The fact that all the independent African states became

founding members of the OAU was important for a number of reasons; first because it showed the underlying unity of purpose spelled out in its charter between the more conservative leaders like Emperor Haile Selassie and President Houphouet-Boingy and the young radicals like President Kwame Nkrumah of Ghana and President Sékou Touré of Guinea; and second, because it rejected the old colonial division between the Arab peoples north of the Sahara and the Black peoples to the south. The OAU's membership affirmed that the Sahara was not a political barrier dividing the continent. Colonel Nasser of Egypt, President Ben Bella of Algeria, King Hassan of Morocco, and President Habib Bourguiba of Tunisia showed that they had less in common with each other than with their conservative and radical counterparts in Sub-Saharan Africa.

Pan-Africanism embraces a number of themes which found their echo in the liberation struggle. They include the rejection of Black inferiority and demand for equality; insistence on recognizing the dignity of Black people; pride in Blackness—"Black is Beautiful," and Black Consciousness. After a visit to Africa, Langston Hughes wrote:

> I am a Negro,
> Black as the night is black,
> Black like the depths of my Africa.[6]

Pan-African ideology is careful to distinguish between race-consciousness and racism. Black Consciousness, as defined by two South African martyrs—Robert Sobukwe and Steve Biko—recognizes only one race—the human race. The influence of cultural diversity is shown by the differences between the Anglophone and Francophone expressions of Black Consciousness. The French movement—largely inspired by men like Senghor, the Martiniquan poet and politician Aimé Césaire, and Leon Delmas—developed a concept of Negritude which reflects with Cartesian and

23

Marxist methods of analysis. Senghor described it as *racisme* vs. *racisme*. The ideology adopts a thesis, antithesis, synthesis mode. The thesis posits pride in the Black race; the antithesis rejects White racism; finally, a synthesis is achieved between them. This kind of analysis was frequently assailed by Anglophone Pan-Africanists, but in the end, there is really no difference in either the practice or the outcome. Nevertheless, such controversies added excitement to the intellectual exchanges of the 1960s; these dialogues were further stirred by Frantz Fanon's ideas about the place of violence in "decolonizing the mind," upon which he expounded in *The Wretched of the Earth*.

The romantic views about the shape and needs of the postcolonial nation-state reflected the experience of the modern industrial nations. Africa's economic growth, it was argued, had been retarded by colonial exploitation and concentration on mining and the development of cash crops like cocoa, groundnuts, coffee, tea, and sisal; the priority set for the new state was building up primary and secondary industry, mass education and technical training, and improving health facilities.

Although many leaders of the postcolonial states were initially hostile to trans-nationals,[7] Nkrumah signed an agreement with the American industrialist Henry Kaiser to build a large aluminum factory based on a modern hydroelectric plant on the Volta Dam. He also established a new industrial area at Tema, and sought to attract investors and entrepreneurs from around the world. Many of them turned out to be crooks. The height of this folly of planning the rapid industrialization of African countries was the blueprint prepared by the Marxist Planning Minister for Mozambique, which envisaged a "Ruhr type" of heavy industrial development for his war-ravaged country. It turned out to be more Ruritanian than Ruhr.

The ambitious schemes by the modernizing elites

involved allocating large quantities of scarce resources to urban areas. Rural neglect remained and was even enhanced. Unrelieved peasant poverty was the price paid for this heavy concentration on the modern sector, on a greatly expanded civil service, and a larger and better equipped army with standards of pay and privileges for the top ranks mimicking those of the expatriate officer class.

Suddenly, Africa found itself inundated with offers of financial aid from all over the industrial world, including international financial institutions and commercial banks. Hungry for development and as yet lacking the local expertise or institutions to ensure either the efficient and honest application of the loans to priority projects, or to increase productivity, the largesse turned out to be a poisoned chalice.

For centuries, even before colonialism, Africans had little opportunity to learn about their continent, or about each other. Now the new nationalist leaders began for the first time to get to know each other, and to meet and plan their continent's future. A small number had met together for the first time at the end of World War I at the 1919 Pan-African Congress in Paris; a more representative group gathered at the seminal 1945 Pan-African Congress in Manchester; but the growing excitement of these meetings reached a new pitch when delegates from all over the continent met in December in 1958 in Accra, the capital of the first SSA independent state, where the all-African People's Congress brought together scores of still-unknown politicians who were to gain prominence in the years ahead.[8]

The Accra meeting was followed by a series of conferences organized by the new rival grouping that had begun to emerge reflecting the divisions between African leaders—the conservative Monrovia Group and the mostly radical members of the Casablanca Group. Those in the West and the Soviet bloc who had predicted that the emergent African states would split the continent between conservatives and radicals were proved wrong when all the African leaders came together in Addis Ababa in May 1963 to launch the Organization of African Unity (OAU).

Some leaders of independent countries also appeared for the first time at international gatherings, such as the Bandung conference in 1955, where the seeds were planted for the non-alignment movement.

Paralleling these meetings of political leaders were gatherings of African professionals, artists, and writers. In 1960, one hundred and ninety-four African lawyers and jurists met in Nigeria, where they issued the Law of Lagos, proclaiming their commitment to human rights and the Rule of Law; writers and artists from all over Africa and the diaspora met at two conferences of "Negro Writers and Artists" in Paris in 1956 and Rome in 1959.

Ebullient, extroverted, and confident, Africa was bursting out of its pre-colonial chrysalis in the aftermath of the Second World War into a new era of Cold War politics.

One friend of African independence had sadly surveyed the shifting economic priorities and interests of the new ruling class, and the rise of a burgeoning bureaucracy. The man was René Dumont, a French agronomist who wrote the epitaph to the romantic period in his book *False Start in Africa*.[9] "Independence," he wrote, "was not always decolonization." Criticizing the new elites, he pointed out that a deputy (M.P.) earned as much in six weeks as did an average peasant in thirty-six years. But in the heady days of the first decade of independence, the counsels of this savant found little response. Africa was on its way, shouting new slogans: *Freedom* in West Africa, *Uhuru* in the East, and *Amandla* in the South. By the end of 1980, all of Africa, except for Guinea-Bissau, was independent as far south as the Zambezi. By then, too, the pressures were beginning to tell on the Portuguese colonies, and a last-ditch attempt was made to halt the march to emancipation in Rhodesia,

THE ROMANTIC PERIOD, 1939–1970

where the Smith regime made a desperate Unilateral Declaration of Independence (UDI). Only the apartheid system in South Africa and Namibia still stood firm, as the strong and last redoubts of the counterrevolution.

Six men held the stage in the first decade of the romantic period—Kwame Nkrumah and Jomo Kenyatta, followed by Tom Mboya and Julius Nyerere in English-speaking Africa and Leopold Senghor and Felix Houphouet-Boigny in the Francophone countries.

Nkrumah was for a time the hope of the continent. Young, handsome, charismatic, controversial, fresh from Lincoln University in the United States, he set a new agenda for Africa, including the creation of what he called the reborn "African personality"—independent, proud, and honest. He set himself up as the crusading leader for the political unification and liberation of Africa. "No country will be free until all of Africa is free," he said in his inaugural speech as president on 6 March 1957. He preached socialism, but was ambiguous about Marxism. C. L. R. James, the famous West Indian Marxist (Fourth International), cricket writer, and Shakespearean, summed up Nkrumah's influence: "To the Africans and people of African descent everywhere, the name Nkrumah became for many years a symbol of release from the subordination to which they had been subjected for so many centuries. Kwame Nkrumah was one of the greatest political leaders of our century." He died alone in exile in Bucharest, having been overthrown on 24 February 1966, nine years after his election as president. He owed his downfall partly to his own faults, partly because he had become entrapped in the Cold War. Like other charismatic leaders through the ages, he had built a cult of personality around himself— Osagyefo, the Great Warrior. He introduced a notorious Preventive Detention Act to imprison opponents indefinitely and without trial. To promote his ideas for the liberation of Africa, he declared war on conservative leaders like

Houphouet-Boigny and sponsored subversive activities to undermine their regimes. A variety of reasons, external and internal, led to a sharp decline in Ghana's economy. Although Nkrumah frequently assailed the spread of corruption, he failed to act against it, possibly because so many of his close associates were involved. Finally, disenchanted with the West, he reluctantly drew closer to Moscow—a fatal blunder, since his increasingly strong internal opposition was able to get the CIA involved in the planning of his overthrow by force. His mistakes and misdeeds are now largely over-looked or forgotten, and the name Nkrumah continues to inspire new generations of Africans.

Tom Mboya of Kenya was perhaps the most clever young politician of Africa in the 1960s. His brilliant mind was matched by an electrifying personality. The popularity of a young Luo politician who happened not to be a Kikuyu caused jealousies among the dominant Kikuyu in the camp of President Jomo Kenyatta, but also from the older Luo leader, "Double O," Oginga Odinga. Mboya's assassination before the age of forty robbed the continent of the kind of talent that had begun to develop only in the nascent years of the new Africa.

Jomo Kenyatta was a towering figure in Kenya. He was the first East African to challenge White settler rule. When he chose exile in England, he studied anthropology under the distinguished Professor Malinowski at the London School of Economics and wrote an important book, *Facing Mount Kenya*. He played a controversial role in the Mau Mau uprising, for which he was imprisoned. Although branded as a communist and a dangerous radical, after becoming the country's first president, he proved himself to be a conservative (much admired by the settler community) and a Kikuyu chauvinist. His regime was clouded by corruption.

Julius Nyerere, the third of the trio of young African leaders, stood closer to Mboya than to Nkrumah, though

THE ROMANTIC PERIOD, 1939-1970

he admired both. Of the three, he seems destined to leave the most enduring legacy: the only successful agrarian revolution in Africa. While the idealistic side of his policy—creating cooperative peasant villages—failed, the transformation of traditional rural life with its scattered individual peasant homesteads into communities living in consolidated rural villages has laid a permanent foundation for improving the quality of rural life—more and better schools, health clinics, piped fresh water, and the availability of more technical help to improve farming methods.

Houphouet-Boigny, the president of the Côte d'Ivoire, was the grand old man of Francophone Africa, a romantic conservative who devoted much of his life and of his country's resources to creating a sparkling new city center in his home town, Yamousoukro, built a marble palace to rival the finest in Europe, a cathedral with measurements larger than St. Peter's, and an irrigated modern farm to inspire others. He bears a remarkable resemblance to the aristocrats of Renaissance Europe. He was also an astute politician who believed that Africa's true independence lay in following the capitalist path. He and Nkrumah represented the two opposite political poles. Houphouet once wagered Nkrumah that in ten years his country would be better off than Ghana. Depending on how one measures "better-off," Houphouet will seem to have won.

However, it is Nkrumah, and not Houphouet, who has left a durable heritage. Some of his ideas, if not his practices, continue to live but, above all, the Organization of African Unity (OAU)—though not in the form he wished it to take—stands as a memorial to Nkrumah's espousal of Pan-Africanism. Interestingly, Houphouet never attended a single summit of the OAU, not even when it was held almost next door in Liberia. The reason always given for his nonattendance was his reluctance to fly, but this reluctance did not stop him from flying, usually twice a year, to

Paris, and once even more widely in Europe in a futile attempt to bring back his beautiful young wife, who had left him.

Leopold Senghor, Senegal's first president, qualified for the pejorative description of a "Black Frenchman." Struggling as he did to recover his African roots, it is not surprising that this poet-politician should have been prominent in formulating the dialectical ideas of Negritude. He seemed more at home in the political and intellectual circles of Paris than in the provincial milieu of his own capital, Dakar. When he retired as president, he chose to spend his last years living in France.

THE ROMANTIC PERIOD, 1939-1970

TWO

The Period of Disillusionment, 1970–1985

'Tis all in pieces
All coherence gone.
—John Donne

The Nigerian writer Chinua Achebé's novel *Things Fall Apart* captured the mood of disillusionment that settled over postindependence Africa for much of the twenty years between the early 1970s and the middle 1980s. The dream of a Golden Age had withered on the tender vine of independence, and it became clear that Africa was not going to escape the experience of Europe, the Americas, and Asia in comparable historical periods when they were evolving and consolidating their new nation-states. The historical process of creating nation-states has passed through similar stages and encountered many similar problems worldwide. An examination of Africa's history in the latter half of the twentieth century shows that many of the factors which destroyed the optimism of the period of romanticism in Africa were not very different from those in Europe—which had experienced its Hundred Years' War, Napoleonic conquest, assassinations, times of chaos, conflicts over borders, and civil war in the consolidation of the evolving new states. It was similar, too, in the Americas, with the fratricidal killings and the bitterness of the American Civil War; the racism of slavery; the corruption and miseries of the Reconstruction years; and in Latin America, where a succession of wars was fought over the shaping of borders; the rise of dictators and military regimes; oppression and the widespread abuses of the human rights of the indigenous populations; internal conflicts; the collapse of institutions; and the failure of Simon Bolivar's ambition to unify Latin America.

Two major differences were that the wars and revolutions in Europe and the Americas exceeded in scale and casualties the violent episodes in Africa, bad as these were; and that the latter period of the consolidation of the nation-states in Europe and America was also a time of rapid economic growth, partly due to the exploitation of colonial resources. Such a perspective serves to show that the African experience was not unique or especially "African." Another main difference between the African experience and the rest of the world is that the birth of nation-states occurred almost two centuries later in Africa, at a time when communications, technology, and trade had created an international community in which no country or continent was screened off from the rest of the world.

Between 1966 and 1993, there were sixty-three military coups in Africa and twenty-four violent conflicts. Of these, only four reached the proportions of a full-scale war involving extra-continental powers (Algeria, Angola, Mozambique, and Ethiopia). Four more had the character of armed guerrilla struggles (Rhodesia, Namibia, South Africa, and Eritrea). Two were cross-border attacks (Somalia into Ethiopia, and Tanzania into Uganda; the Mali-Niger encounter was a minor affair). There was only one true, successful revolution (Zanzibar). In Ethiopia, Mengistu Haile Mariam, in alliance with the USSR, attempted a Marxist revolution (which became stalled). One was genocidal (Rwanda). The rest were civil wars—the most serious were those in Sudan, Nigeria, Liberia, Somalia, Burundi, and Ethiopia. Of these, only four—the Biafra war, the conflict between Ethiopia and Eritrea, and the internecine fighting in Rwanda and Burundi—were predominantly ethnic. The horrific ongoing war in Sudan is essentially religious, regional, and political. It is not just a conflict between the non-Muslim South and the predominantly Muslim North, since the two powerful Islamic sects (the Ansaris and Khatmia) are opposed to the fundamentalist Muslim regime.

Between 1966 and 1993, about ten million people lost their lives and at least five times as many were wounded in African conflicts. More than twenty million became refugees or were displaced from their homes in their own country.

THE RISE OF MILITARY REGIMES

The phenomenon of military coups leading to violent conflict is not peculiar to Africa; coups have played a destabilizing role in many Asian countries (including Pakistan, Indonesia, Burma, and Thailand), and have been a recurring feature of political change in South America. What has been peculiar to African coups is their frequency and the ease of their success, mostly bloodless or with minimal loss of life. Except in two cases—Idi Amin in Uganda, and Leading Sergeant Samuel Doe in Liberia—all the other coups were led by officers of the modernizing elites; even the notorious "Emperor" Bokassa of the Central African Republic had been an officer in the French army. The members of the officer class had similar backgrounds to those in the civilian regimes they overthrew, and were often related to them.

The frequency of the military coup was symptomatic of the failure of the post-independence institutions which suffered from such weaknesses as inadequate checks and balances between the executive, legislative, administrative, and judicial branches; a lack of accountability and transparency; and the absence of an influential countervailing civil society. Although armies were, on the whole, relatively small, the military were much the strongest and most coherent power groups in all African countries. They usually acted only when a substantial part of the electorate had become either actively hostile or been reduced to passivity and were fed up with their government; so the military often emerged as the white knight in two kinds of situations: when a government was deadlocked by rival groups within it; or at a time of economic hardship worsened by evidence of corruption and gross human rights abuses.

Both these situations need a brief analysis before considering the failure of military regimes to perform better than civilian rulers.

The deadlock or paralysis in the early post-independence period was usually due to two developments. The first was that, with only a few exceptions (notably Botswana, Namibia, and Tanganyika), all anticolonial liberation movements had become divided before independence, or the victorious ones became split, on average, two to three years after coming to power. The reason for this was that the successful liberation movements were, without exception, united fronts of political and economic interests ranging from the far Right to the extreme Left and were, mostly, broadly representative of major ethnic communities and regions. They united because they shared a common enemy— the colonial power. Once the major aim of defeating the colonial power was achieved, the conflicting interests of the different components of the united front surfaced in the new cabinet over such issues as the distribution of resources between ethnic groups and regions; the direction of economic policy—capitalist or socialist; priority between the public and private sector; foreign policy orientation; as well as the normal kind of power struggles between politicians. Another reason for deadlock in the cabinet was the failure to get agreement on a coalition of all the major political parties to form a national government at independence. Here are some examples of both these causes of breakdown.

Ghana's successful liberation movement, the Convention Peoples Party (CPP), included three political tendencies: Nkrumah's socialist wing; Kojo Botsio's centrist group; and K. A. Gbedemah's right wing, which strongly favored private enterprise. When Nkrumah began to give way under pressures from his more militant left (the so-called Spark group), Gbedemah left the government and became a political challenger to the CPP at a time when the influential opposition Brong-Asanti National Liberation Movement, led by the doyen conservative, Dr. J. B. Danquah, was mounting a serious destabilizing campaign. Gbedemah's defection also intensified the discontent among his community, the Ewe. Soon, defections from the CPP, growing economic discontent and strikes, several attacks on Nkrumah's life, and arrests under a notorious Preventive Detention Act, weakened the government's authority. Other factors included increasing corruption and the intrusion of Cold War politics.

The other example comes from Nigeria. At independence, there were three major regionally based parties: the Hausa-

Fulani Northern People's Party (NPP), led by Sardauna of Sokoto and Abubakr Tafawa Balewa; the mainly Ibo-based Nigeria and Cameroon National Council (NCNC), led by the nationalist Nnamdi Azikiwe; and the Yoruba-based Action Group, led by Chief Obafemi Awolowo. Despite determined attempts by the prime minister, Abubakr Balewa, to persuade Awolowo to join a coalition government with the NPP and the NCNC, he refused, leaving the government at independence uneasily balanced on two legs of a tripod power base. The decision of one of Awolowo's lieutenants, S. L. Akintola, to break with the Action Group resulted in internecine fighting among the Yoruba, while pressures on Abubakr Balewa were intensified by the more conservative leader of his party, the Sardauna of Sokoto, who was against coalition politics. The unraveling of power at the center led to violence in the Yoruba region, while the NPP's incitement against Ibos working in the North resulted in murderous attacks which triggered the Biafra war.

The military—usually underpaid except for the top hierarchy—sometimes acted from selfish motives to obtain a much bigger slice of the cake for themselves and the army; more often, they acted out of what they perceived as a sense of duty to prevent the collapse of the new state, to break the deadlock in government, or to deal with corruption. On a few occasions, their motivation was to change the political system, as in the case of two coups in the Sudan, and the coup led by Mengistu Haile Mariam in Ethiopia. But whatever the professed aims of the soldiers, all but two of the military regimes (led by General Obasanjo in Nigeria and Jerry Rawlings in Ghana) ended in almost the same state as the regimes they had supplanted, or even worse: corrupt, internally divided, a centralized bureaucratic form of government, and an economy in a perilous state of decline. (It is still too soon to definitely

THE PERIOD OF DISILLUSIONMENT, 1970-1985

evaluate Yoweri Museveni's "No party" regime in Uganda.)

Because the military had no previous experience of government, they relied heavily on public servants. In fact, the typical military regime was a partnership between soldiers and public servants. One unfortunate result of this was that the public service became as discredited, and often as corrupt, as the military. Often, too, the judiciary lost its independence, and many judges became corrupt or puppets of the new regimes. Among the frequent outcomes of military regimes were the undermining and discrediting of all the major institutions associated with a democratic state and the neutering of civil society. No show of public discontent through the ballot box, the media, or peaceful demonstrations became possible; human rights were widely abused; education and the social services were run down further, and poverty continued to grow.

TRIBALISM AND ETHNICITY

Westerners describe European conflicts such as the fighting between Serbs, Croats, and Muslim Bosnians as "ethnic conflicts," but similar conflicts in Africa are invariably described as "tribal conflicts." What is the difference? Historian Eric Hobsbawm has argued that ethnicity, whatever its basis, is a readily definable way of expressing a real sense of group identity which links the members of "we" because it emphasizes their difference from "them."[10] How is that different from describing tribal loyalties? How, then, explain the Western habit of referring to "tribalism" and not "ethnicity" when speaking or writing about African conflicts? Why do politicized Africans react angrily against the use of "tribalism"? The answer is really straightforward.

Although the term "tribe" was used in biblical times as connoting self-contained autonomous groups, with the spread of colonialism in the twentieth century, "tribalism"

came to be associated with savagery, barbarism, primitivism, and even cannibalism. Since modern Europeans are
rarely described as "primitive," no matter how barbaric
their behavior, their struggles for autonomy, sovereignty,
or supremacy are not ascribed to "tribalism." It is this asso-
ciation between "tribalism" and primitivism that offends
Africans and which precluded its use in the nationalists'
anticolonial debate. Another reason for rejecting use of the
term was that among the reasons given by the colonial
powers for delaying the granting of independence was that
"tribalism" would make it difficult, if not impossible, to
create stable states in Africa. The anticolonial movement's
answer to this argument was that only through nationalism could supra-tribal loyalties be created without dero-
gating from kinship feelings and loyalties.

Sidestepping the ongoing controversies between histori-
ans, anthropologists, and political scientists over the nature
of ethnicity, tribalism, and nationalism, I prefer a simple
definition for political analysis: at the lowest level of kinship loyalty and social organization is the clan; although
clans often fight each other, they also combine against a
common enemy (*vide* the Scottish and Somali clans); clans
combine over time to form stronger social organizations—
such as district or sub-tribal groups which, reacting to various needs and pressures, tend to coalesce into regional
tribal communities, ethnically linked by a similar history,
a common language, and shared traditional social and religious beliefs. Ethnicity, therefore, is only a higher state of
social and political organizations of tribally linked groups.
In present-day Africa, there are still hundreds of social
communities not yet integrated into larger kinship societies, while many, if not most, tribal societies share a common ethnic loyalty.

The post-independence nation-building experience in
Africa—a subject for serious comparative study—differed
widely. The few relatively homogeneous countries, such as

Lesotho, Botswana, Swaziland, and Somalia, had few difficulties in establishing loyalty to the new state, despite acute political differences in Lesotho and Somalia and less serious problems in Botswana. This also was the case in Mauritius, notwithstanding the sharp differences in the large Hindu community and the wide gulf between them and the small French-speaking community of Creoles. Tanzania was the outstanding success story in creating national loyalty among its one hundred and fifty-six tribes, a success attributable to President Nyerere's tolerant policies and the unifying role of the country's political system. However, ethnic homogeneity is not an absolute guarantee of national unity. Although the Somalis are in every sense a nation—with their own language, a shared religion (100 percent Muslim), and adherence to historic, though mobile, territorial boundaries—they have maintained a largely traditional system of rival nomadic clans competing for scarce water and grazing land resources. When the narrow coalition of clans that formed the regime of Siad Barre broke up, clan warfare broke out which not only resulted in the secession of the northern clans but threatened the state itself.

Some ascribe the Tanzanian success to the fact that the country had established a single-party system soon after independence; but a multi-party political system, as in Ghana, produced a common loyalty to the nation's new flag in spite of a serious, at times violent, challenge to Kwame Nkrumah's government by the Brong–Asanti Confederacy's long-established monarchical and other institutions. The experience was again different in Uganda, where the Buganda Kingdom at first threatened secession and later demanded autonomy—a challenge which caused the country's first post-independence crisis. At independence, Zambia faced a similar challenge to its unity from the Paramount Chieftaincy of Barotseland, but opposition to the traditional leadership by a small modernizing elite among the territory's Lozis helped to blunt the threat of secession.

Some countries—notably Kenya—suffered a long period of instability because at independence the country's strongest ethnic community, the Kikuyu, in alliance with smaller tribes, marginalized the second largest ethnic community, the Luo. Ethnic cleavages that had been unsolved at independence continued to destabilize countries like Rwanda and Burundi (between Hutus and Tutsis); Mauritania (between the Muslim Arabs and the non-Muslim Negro riverine community; and the Sudan (between the Muslim Arab North and the mainly non-Muslim Negro South). Other countries achieved a large measure of unity but failed to accommodate the demands of regional groups, e.g. the Casamance region of Senegal; the Anglophone Northerner territory of the Cameroon; and the Tuaregs in Niger and Mali. Some of the ethnic and other problems of Nigeria have been discussed above.

Some of the most serious conflicts in the continent occurred when ethnic loyalties were mobilized to advance particularist causes. Examples of this were Colonel Ojukwu's rallying of the Ibos in the Biafra war; Dr. Jonas Savimbi's mobilization of the Ovimbundu in the civil war in Angola; Moise Tshombe's near-success in winning local support for Katanga's secession from the Congo Republic shortly after independence; Joshua Nkomo's leadership of the Ndebele in his power struggle with Robert Mugabe's Shona-led regime; and Chief Gatsha Buthelezi's Zulu-based Inkatha Freedom Party in opposition to the African National Congress (ANC). Incidentally, the idea of impermeable homogeneity did not hold up in the case of the Zulus when some 40 percent of the community voted for the ANC in the 1994 general elections. Another example is the disunity of the Amharas in Ethiopia in the 1992 elections.

While ethnicity-based problems obstructed the nation-building process in postcolonial Africa and were a major cause of political instability, experience differed widely across the continent. An interesting postscript to this brief summary is the first democratic constitution in Ethiopia, which provides for a federation of ethnic states.

Promoting and preserving national unity has been expensive and frequently called for repressive measures. Everyone is not agreed that the result justifies the cost. One dissident view has been expressed by a group of Cameroonian intellectuals:

> The only evident result of the thirty years of national unity in the name of which our governments have forgotten the security and the liberty of its citizens and sacrificed economic development of the nation, is an open and permanent invitation to each ethnic group to struggle, especially to the exclusion of merit, by cheating, by fraud and with impunity to place its proteges in power in order to guarantee themselves a portion of the national cake.[11]

THE QUESTION OF CORRUPTION

Although corruption is universal, seriously affecting even long-established, rich, and democratic societies, it is a particular phenomenon with special characteristics in most, if not all, newly emerging independent states, or in states where power has shifted from one political or social class to another. This particular phenomenon may be attributed to a variety of factors, some of which are described below.

Many leaders of a new political class, holding power for the first time, come from deprived homes and communities; their families often exert a strong influence on them for favorable treatment. Acquiring smart clothes, Gucci shoes, and expensive leather briefcases—extravagances beyond their incomes—marks the importance of the arriviste. The opportunities for acquiring possessions previously available only to the former ruling class or wealthy old families is often irresistible. This, too, has been true in different periods of development in now-rich countries, as is made evident by the rapid accumulation of wealth of a new class of petit bourgeoisie and through pork-barrel politics. The nouveau riche everywhere is notoriously greedy and takes delight in the ostentatious display of its new wealth. Many of the newly rich have a psychological greed for more wealth than is necessary for several lifetimes of good living, as may be seen among those already wealthy: millionaires who want to become billionaires, and billionaires who strive to become multi-billionaires—a psychological obsession seen all over the world. Kenyans saw it displayed in the speed with which the Kenyatta family acquired farms, buildings, and directorships after independence—an example followed by Kenyatta's successor, Daniel arap Moi— but even these excesses were outclassed by the raping of Zaire's treasures by Mobutu, who not only built a Renaissance palace in Gbadolite, but also bought prestigious chalets in Belgium, France, and Switzerland, à la the Ramos family in the Philippines.

There is also a more reasonable explanation for the misuse of office by members of the new political class who cannot be certain of their tenure in the unstable conditions of a new state. Hence the temptation to "make hay while the sun shines" felt by civil servants, politicians, and party officials who often feel insecure in their positions. Also, political parties and politicians need funds to maintain their organizations and secure the chances for their own reelection.

Here are a few examples of the beginnings of corruption in two new African states which I personally observed. Within the first few weeks of independence in Ghana, Nkrumah's CPP used public funds to buy an old cinema for something like £30,000 but gave the sale price as £100,000. The difference was paid into the party's funds. Since the CPP needed to build up a strong party machinery to entrench its position, this widely known deal did not seem so outrageous at the time. Next, Nkrumah discovered that some of his ministers were accepting payoffs from foreign building firms for contracts. Instead of cracking down on this practice, which would not have gone down well with some of his colleagues, Nkrumah institutionalized payoffs by declaring that 10 percent of all bribes were to be paid over to the party. This opened the way for extensive bribe-taking in Ghana, which is known to have been resisted by only one senior minister, Kofi Baako.

My next example comes from Nigeria, where, almost from the beginning of independence, a thrusting entrepreneurial class engaged in sophisticated scams. For example, the finance minister, having established his own shoe factory, introduced a heavy tariff on the import of shoes. An outraged public figure once provided me with a large file of documents containing evidence of corrupt deals with the request that I should hand the file over to the prime minister, Abubakr Tafawa Balewa, known for his honesty. My whistle-blower thought that the dossier of corruption would carry more weight coming from a foreign journalist. Many of the allegations were against the hugely corrupt finance minister. As I began to go through the documents in the dossier with the prime minister, I noticed him pressing a bell to speak to his private secretary, whom he addressed in Hausa. The secretary soon returned carrying a very fat file. "Mr. Legum," Abubakr said. "My file of complaints against the finance minister is much greater than yours. My trouble is that the minister is a powerful figure in his area and is indispensable to my efforts to establish a coalition government." (Both men were killed in the 1966 coup which brought in the first of a succession of military regimes, each more corrupt than the previous one.) Nigeria, Zaire, and Kenya did not just develop corrupt governments, they spawned corrupt societies—an infinitely more difficult situation to rectify.

It has become an unfortunate practice in the Western media to write sweepingly of "corrupt African leaders and governments," ignoring the role of leaders like Julius Nyerere, Nelson Mandela, Milton Obote, Kenneth Kaunda, Leopold Senghor, and others who have stood out against the corruption in their own governments. Nyerere, for example, retired with only his pension and a donated bungalow; Obote was driven penniless into exile in Zambia, where he lives almost in penury in a guest-house and with food provided by the government.

REASONS FOR THE ECONOMIC DECLINE

By 1986, the population of Sub-Saharan Africa was, on average, poorer than it had been a decade earlier. By then, of the world's thirty-two developing countries classified as severely indebted low-income countries, twenty-five were in Africa. The declines in most African economies are ascribable to the failure to develop independent postcolonial economies and to both internal and external economic factors. The internal causes were of two kinds—natural forces and mistaken government policies. The latter include a policy of favoring the modern urban economy at the expense of rural areas and concentrating on cash crops for export rather than the production of food which, together with recurrent droughts, ravages of locusts, internal conflicts, and the uprooting of populations, produced the situation foreseen by René Dumont in *False Start in Africa.*

By 1980, the continent was no longer able to feed itself and was forced to import 25 percent of its food needs and to rely on food aid. The heavy expense of importing staple food meant using up valuable foreign earnings, which otherwise could have been used as capital for internal development. Between 1948 and 1966, total agricultural production achieved an average annual growth rate of only 2.44 percent.

The performance of the food and livestock sub-sector was even worse—only 1.6 percent per annum—while the population growth was, on average, 3 percent per annum. Many of the policies implemented by governments in attempts to increase productivity and halt the national economic decline were counter-productive—such as state control of marketing boards and national producer co-operatives; withholding the full world price of primary products from peasant growers; and the establishment of parastatal companies to take over nationalized sectors of the economy.

Parastatals are enterprises set up by the state but given a measure of autonomy which separates them from the civil service. Sometimes they might be in partnership with private companies. Parastatals have, for instance, run electricity and public transport systems, agro-industrial enterprises, and agricultural co-operatives. The parastatals, with few exceptions, not only were themselves a failure but had a negative effect on production, distorted the market, and were partly responsible for higher prices that fed inflation. Many of them became non-accountable centers of power and nepotism, deeply corrupt and inefficient. Some became so strong that governments had difficulty in controlling them. For example, when the government of Mali proposed to abolish its forty parastatals, it encountered such strong opposition that it had to put off its proposed reforms. The establishment of parastatals and other forms of state control are generally presented as socialist policies because of the element of nationalization in setting them up. However, an informed analysis of the difference between socialist planning and the structure of the parastatals shows that the latter resemble state corporations rather than socialist institutions. What became evident too late was that the first generation of independence leaders had, in their understandable wish to free their economies from foreign control, embarked on policies that created non-democratic, non-accountable, and non-transparent institutions at the heart of the economy.

Turning to the external causes of economic decline, the first to consider is the impact of the debt burden and its progenitor—foreign aid. To this day, more capital wealth (profits mainly from mining, much of it in repayment and redemption of foreign loans) is transferred every year to the industrialized world than is received through an inward flow of foreign aid and capital. There has been, and still is, a very low level of private capital investment except in the oil sector and more recently in mining development.

As mentioned earlier, in the first flush of independence, the young governments had been easily tempted by lavish offers of foreign aid, which they saw as a means of stimu-lating development and financing education and health infrastructure programs. While aid on reasonable terms can contribute to development, the necessary condition is that the loans should produce more than the interest and redemption costs. This did not happen, with the result that by the end of the 1980s, most Sub-Saharan countries were forced to devote anything between 40 percent and 82 per-cent of their foreign exchange earnings to redeeming their foreign debt. The total debt burden of the twenty-five poor-est countries was approaching $200 billion, 24 percent of it owed to multilateral institutions, and the balance made up of bilateral (government to government) and commercial loans. The debt service to export goods and services was around 200 percent. Debt thus became one of the major obstacles to Africa's development.

Another adverse external factor is the imbalance in world trade, which allows powerful consumer nations to fix commodity prices to suit their own interests. Apart from primary producing countries not knowing from one year to the next what contribution their export earnings will make to their budgets, there has been a steady drop in the world market price of most commodities and many

46

minerals. As an example, ten years after Tanganyika's independence it took eight times as many tons of coffee to buy a tractor as it had to import the same size and make of tractor at the time of independence.

Two more crippling blows struck the struggling economy of the Sub-Saharan states. The first was the tripling and quadrupling of oil prices in 1973. Developing countries had to pay twice for the oil price hike—first, they had to pay the higher cost of fuel and fertilizer imports; and second, they had to pay the higher cost of imported industrial goods, whose price was raised at their source in the industrial countries to take account of the rise in energy costs. These increased prices raised transport costs, which is a crucial factor in the great distances traveled between the ports and the interior in vast African countries, while oil for tractors and fertilizers for crops became prohibitively expensive. The higher bills for oil imports critically affected the balance of payments, already strained by the food imports needed by most countries. 1973 was therefore a critical year for the economy of most African countries. Even worse was to come with the Great Drought Disaster of 1983-1985. By then, the food self-sufficiency ratio had dropped progressively from 98 percent in the 1960s to 86 percent in 1980 and 75 percent in 1985-1986. For a people who, at independence, received only 90 percent of their nutritional requirements per day, the drought disaster brought famine and disease to hundreds of thousands.[12]

At the end of the period reviewed in this chapter, African economies were affected by World Bank and IMF policies and by the new ideology of globalization. This will be considered in the next chapter. A number of other developments contributed to the climate of disillusionment. The high rate of population increase—an average of at least 3 percent in most countries and as high as 3.3 percent in Kenya—at a time when the economic growth rate varied between 1 percent and 2 percent—meant a negative growth rate, so less funding was available for education and for health services at a time when the AIDS pandemic was infecting between 4 percent and 10 percent of many SSA populations. (In 1997, according to the World Health Organization's report for 1998, of the estimated 12–13 million people infected by AIDS worldwide, 50 percent were in Africa.) Tuberculosis—the second biggest killer—began to increase; and a new strain of deadly malaria made its appearance in 1989, at a time when 1.5 million children under the age of five were already dying of malaria. Diarrhea was killing an equal number of young children.

The further impoverishment of the rural areas led to a rapid increase in the size of urban populations. Cities like Kinshasa, Lagos, Khartoum, and Nairobi exploded tenfold within a few years, creating all the problems associated with urban squalor and crime. Unemployment in Africa rose from 7.7 percent in 1978 to 22.8 percent in 1990 and is projected to reach 30 percent by the turn of the century. The Economic Commission for Africa predicted that Africa's urban population will increase almost two and a half times between now and 2025, from the present 201 million to 468 million. Compare this urban population of almost 500 million with the continent's present total population of 650 million. The time was approaching when it would be realistic to ask whether the larger African cities would become ungovernable—a glimpse of which had already been seen in Soweto and other South African cities, where popular discontent with the apartheid system became manifest.

What role has the Organization of African Unity (OAU) played during this developing crisis? It had contributed largely to the defeat of the Smith regime in Rhodesia and to the abdication of Portugal's centuries-old rule in Africa by its support for the liberation movements and through international pressures. It also contributed to the international campaign to isolate the apartheid regime. However, it failed in one of its major aims—to create five economic regions within the continent as the nucleus of a continent-wide economic system to overcome Africa's balkanized economies. It succeeded in preventing any serious border conflicts and limiting the effects of the few that occurred. But it failed to intervene in serious internal conflicts affecting its member-states because of its charter's prohibition of such intervention. However, in 1990 this prohibition was changed and elaborate machinery established for the prevention of conflicts and conciliation in disputes.

SUMMING UP

During the 1970s, the main characteristic of the African economy was its outward orientation based on its excessive dependence on a limited number of export commodities for which there was little domestic and diminishing external demand.[13] It became a cliché that Africa is a continent that produces what it does not consume, and consumes what it does not produce.

By the end of the 1980s, not much was left of the early romantic dream and hope that greeted the continent's independence, and little was left of democratic parliamentary institutions. By the beginning of the 1990s, forty-two states were under either military or single-party rule, and only five still maintained multiparty systems. Liberation had not brought freedom to the people. Instead of the promise of free democratic political systems, the two or so decades since independence had seen the sprawling growth of the centralized bureaucratic state.

As already mentioned, the nation-state in Africa was born the wrong way round: the colonial regimes had created the centralized state, but had made little contribution toward creating a nation; indeed it was neither in their interests nor in their capacity to do so, if they had attempted such a thing. Nation-building is essentially a function of nationalist forces, usually in reaction to external hostility. It is a historical process that takes decades to change tribal or ethnic loyalties into a shared supra-loyalty to a modern state, and once achieved it is virtually impossible to extinguish. Recent examples of this are the eruption of ethnic politics in the former Soviet Union and Yugoslavia.

Writing of India on the eve of its independence, the poet Tagore said: "It does not need a defeatist to feel deeply anxious about the future of millions when all their innate cultures and peaceful traditions are being simultaneously subjected to hunger, disease, exploitation (foreign and indigenous), and the seething discontents of communalism." Thinking of Africa, we may be deeply anxious, yes, but not defeatist nor depressed, for just as the euphoria of the romantic period was succeeded by a period of disillusionment, so too were there encouraging lessons learned, bringing the promise of a new period of realism.

THE PERIOD OF DISILLUSIONMENT, 1970–1985

THREE

The Period of Realism, 1988–?

*Failure to decolonize meant, in fact, failure to confront the past,
make amends and make repairs. It implies a carry-over of the
diabilities from the slave trade era to the colonial period, and from
the colonial period into the period after independence. This often
involved a loss of self-esteem, an undue willingness to substitute
dependence on charity for self-confidence and self-reliance.*
—*Prof. Ade-Ajayi*[14]

By the beginning of the 1980s, the continent had deterio-
rated to the point, where, according to Sadiq Rasheed of
the Economic Commission for Africa, "an overwhelming
majority of Africans became trapped in a vicious circle of
poverty, hunger, disease, death, displacement, and civil
wars."[15] The following selective figures illustrate this haz-
ardous situation.

No single African country ranks among the top countries listed on the UN Development Programme's Human
Development Index (HDI), an index which measures a
country's development not by orthodox financial criteria,
but by such special factors as the rate of infant mortality,

age expectancy, literacy, employment, and average annual incomes. By these criteria, 77 percent of African countries rank among those in the low human development category; and 83 percent are among the thirty countries with the lowest HDI economic growth rates, which averaged 2 percent in the 1980s, while individual income levels fell by 1 percent a year. They fell even further, by an average of 1.7 percent, during the first four years of the 1990s. What these figures show us is a continent that has been growing poorer year by year. In Sub-Saharan Africa, per capita income fell from $563 in 1980 to $485 in 1993. In 1990, 216 million people were deemed to be living in poverty—a figure projected to rise to 304 million by the year 2000. More than 60 percent of the rural population in Sub-Saharan Africa fell below the poverty line, while empirical studies suggest that poverty among the urban population (now expanded to 10 percent of the total population) is growing rapidly. Those hardest hit by poverty are women and female-headed households; their number has increased by 50 percent in the last twenty years, as compared to a 30 percent increase in the number of households headed by men. Unemployment is estimated to have risen to 22.8 percent between 1978 and 1990, and is projected to rise further to 30 percent by the year 2000. Underemployment is estimated to have risen to 100 million. What is particularly worrying is the growing unemployment among the under-25-year-olds, even among the educated youth. While school enrollment increased from 1965 to a high of 8 percent a year in the 1970s, it plummeted to 2.2 percent in the 1980s. The number of children in primary schools declined by 7 percent to 72 percent due to cuts in public spending. The adult illiteracy rate in East Africa is 24 percent.

Shortages and higher prices of food had a devastating effect on nutrition and health. Between 1980 and 1991, the number of those existing on the minimum of calories

(1,600–1,700) rose by 70 percent from 99 million to 168 million. Of 177 million malnourished children in the world, about 30 million are African.

It is possible to go on and on piling one set of disturbing figures on top of another to make a pyramid of agony, misery, and failure, with suggestions of even worse to come. The World Bank, for example, has predicted that by the year 2000, poverty in the populations of the developing world will be reduced by 400 million, but in Sub-Saharan Africa (except for South Africa) the trend could go the other way, up by 100 million.

If this were the whole picture, it would give cause for real despair: Africa would indeed be a "basket case." But the figures quoted above describe only the darkest side of the scenario. A new trend is reflected in the following developments.

The number of serious violent conflicts has gone down from six wars to one (Sudan); two civil wars (Algeria and Rwanda/Burundi); and three relatively minor armed struggles for power (Congo-Brazzaville, Sierra Leone, and Somalia). Compared to any other period since the mid-1960s, this marks a dramatic advance. The evil apartheid regime was replaced through a bloodless transfer of power by an African majority democratic government headed by an icon, Nelson Mandela, as president. The wars in Angola and Mozambique had ended with the withdrawal of Portugal from the continent. And with the independence of Namibia and Zimbabwe, peace had finally come to the Southern African region. The last of the major corrupt authoritarian figures, Mobutu Sese Seko, had died in defeat and disgrace. In just over a decade, the African revolution of independence, which had been stalled on the Zambezi river, was completed. However, one new area of serious conflict had developed in the Great Lakes region of Central Africa as a result of the resurgence of the Hutu-Tutsi conflict.

Since the end of the 1980s there have been twenty-nine elections contested on a multiparty basis; and though most were more or less seriously flawed, they did allow for organized opposition parties to emerge. Before 1990, there were forty-one military and other types of single-party regimes; by 1996, there were only six military regimes (Nigeria, Rwanda, Burundi, the renamed Congo Democratic Republic [formerly Zaire], and Sierra Leone); one single-party regime (Uganda), and the maverick Libyan regime of Colonel Gadhafi.

Economic recovery has begun: twenty-four countries had growth rates of more than 4 percent in 1996, while thirty-two grew faster in 1995–1996 than in the previous three years. The IMF predicted that the average growth rate (barring climatic disasters) could be back to the average 6 percent growth of the immediate postcolonial period. More than one hundred parastatal companies have been privatized, and a relatively free market system now operates throughout the continent.

The period of realism was slow in arriving, but once it began, it rushed in like a flood from different directions that threatened the non-democratic political systems created by the first generation of independence leaders.

The first defining moment of this new period was when the continent's leaders began to come to grips with the truth of René Dumont's pre-independence warning in *False Start in Africa*. A summit of Africa's leaders, convened in Lagos in 1985 by the OAU, produced a Plan of Action for Food, which opened on a realistic note:

> Over the last two decades, and at a time the African continent is facing a rapid growth in population and urbanization, the food and agriculture situation in Africa has undergone a drastic deterioration; the food production and consumption per person has fallen below nutritional requirements.[16]

THE PERIOD OF REALISM, 1988–?

Five years later, Africa's leaders assembled at an OAU summit, where they confessed that very little progress has been achieved in the implementation of the Lagos Plan (LPA). A resolution adopted on the implementation of the Lagos Plan admitted that although its philosophy, principles, and objectives have been accepted by member-states as a whole, their underlying concerns are not always translated into concrete action or reflected in national development plans.[17]

Among the reasons listed to account for the lack of success were that radical change of the colonial economic structures inherited by most African countries has proven difficult; and that national development plans and annual budgets of most African countries have tended to perpetuate and even accentuate economic dependency through over-reliance on foreign resources (financial and human) and have led to the misallocation of domestic resources through reduction of such high priority areas as agriculture. After the Great Drought Disaster, another African summit adopted Africa's Priority Program for Economic Recovery (APPER), which was later converted into the UN Program of Action for Africa's Economic Recovery and Development (UN-PAAERD), which was followed in 1989 by the African Alternative Framework for Structural Adjustment Programs for Socio-Economic Recovery and Transformation (AAF-SAC), and in 1990 by the African Charter for Popular Participation for Development (ACPPD). All these in-depth analyses of the continent's failures and needs were submitted to the United Nations to enlist international cooperation in rescuing the continent from its critical situation. Although help was promised in principle by major Western countries, it was half-hearted, conditional, and finally jettisoned by the World Bank and International Monetary Fund in favor of their own Structural Adjustment Programs (SAPs) which, for the next ten years, did little to improve Africa's economy and did serious harm to social conditions until the international agencies belatedly began to learn from their mistakes.

Every year, still more capital continues to flow out of Africa to Western Europe, the United States, and Japan than comes into the continent. The outflow is accounted for by interest and redemption of the foreign debt and profits from oil and mining ventures. One figure will suffice to illustrate this inequity: the ratio of foreign debt to Gross Domestic Product (GDP) for Sub-Saharan Africa (excluding South Africa) went up by 25 percent from 102.1 percent in 1991 to 126 percent in 1994, and rose further thereafter. An estimated 70 percent of Africa's private wealth is invested outside the continent, according to Paul Collier, head of the World Bank's research department.[18]

The end of the Cold War brought positive benefits to Africa, but it also had some negative effects. On the positive side was the fact that the Western powers (especially the United States, but also to some extent France, Germany, and England) stopped helping, or harming, African countries depending on "whose side" they were perceived to stand. This change in Western policy, and the end of Russian involvement, contributed to stopping the war in Angola; helped to bring the downfall of the Ethiopian regime of Mengistu Haile Mariam; further reduced support for Mobutu; and, crucially, helped to hasten the end of apartheid. All these developments reduced the climate of violence in the continent, and largely ended Western (particularly United States and French) intervention on the side of favorites at a time when the Second War of Liberation had gotten underway.

The First War of Liberation was fought to gain freedom from alien rule, that is against colonialism and white supremacy in the South; the Second War was against the indigenous rule of the first generation of independence leaders, military regimes, and single-party states—a revolt against what Crawford Young has described as "patrimonial autocracies."[19] It was a struggle for democracy—a continent-wide explosion of anger against the abuse of power, violations of human rights, economic failure, and hardship, and a deep longing for peace and order. As people all over the continent took to the streets, the battle cry they raised was "democracy—one man, one vote."

The Western powers, at first, encouraged the democratic movement by making economic aid conditional on "good governance," which included ending support for single-party states and for regimes guilty of gross abuses of human rights. This policy had two quick results in Kenya and Malawi. However, the policy was applied selectively, and after a few years the Western powers, for reasons of expediency, largely ceased to enforce it—for example, against Uganda, where a military coup leader, Yoweri Museveni, insisted on establishing a "No Party" state—which, in fact, is a euphemism for a single-party regime.

The collapse of communism in the Soviet Union and the liberation of East European states was an added initiative to spur the pro-democracy movement in Africa, but was not its cause, as is sometimes claimed. The democratic liberation movement in Africa had begun several years before Gorbachev's glasnost, and had, of course, begun in South Africa in its armed struggle phase in the 1960s. However, the struggle in South Africa was against white supremacy and not against indigenous Black governments.

The first early success against a single-party regime was achieved in Algeria in 1988 when the Front de la Liberation Nationale (FLN) quickly succumbed to the demand for it to abandon its political monopoly. However, the Algerian experience brought to light the dangers and difficulties when a closed society is opened up to the free interplay of social and political forces. All those Algerian communities and political groups which had been suppressed and felt themselves excluded from the political system combined to defeat the FLN; Liberals, socialists, alienated FLN supporters, and religious groups joined to register votes in a massive rejection of the FLN with the result that the Front Islamique de Salut (FIS) garnered more than twice as many votes as the FLN. But this was not, as is widely believed, a majority for Islamic fundamentalism; it was a vote by all discontented and frustrated Algerians against the FLN.

At its origin, the dominant strand in the FIS was Muslim fundamentalism and opposition to parliamentary democracy. This raised—and still raises—the political and moral dilemma: should an anti-democratic movement be allowed to win power through the use of democratic processes? The FLN decided not, which led to three results. The first was that the actual strength of the FIS shrank in three subsequent elections from over three million to just over one million votes. The second result was the division of the Muslim Front into three groups: a modernist wing, which subscribes to democratic principles; a militant non-violent wing; and an extremist terrorist wing. The third result was the beginning of a chapter of terrible violence launched by the Army of Islamic Salvation, which began murdering those identified as its enemies—liberals, journalists, and secular women—and spreading terror to bring down the government by slaughtering innocent people in villages. This deadly campaign was met with violence from the side of the state, which resorted to undemocratic practices of repression. The question of how to deal effectively with violent fundamentalist movements while maintaining democratic principles and not abusing human rights is one of the most vexatious challenges facing democratic societies—and not just in the Muslim world.

As the Second War of Liberation advanced across the

THE PERIOD OF REALISM, 1988-?

continent, other weaknesses showed up in the opening up of closed societies—particularly the problems of moving directly from authoritarian rule to democratic government.

By the beginning of the 1990s, the number of single-party and military regimes had shrunk from forty-six to thirty-nine—reversing the trend characteristic of the period of disillusionment. But although thirty-nine of the continent's fifty-three states had by then so-called "free elections," that is, elections in which parties competed on the basis of a universal franchise, the outcome could hardly be described as democratic—not even in those countries where the former regimes had been overturned. In fact, only six African countries can even now be categorized as being democratic: Mauritius, Botswana, South Africa, and, arguably, Tunisia and Senegal.

Does this mean either that the Second War of Liberation—the demand for democracy—has failed, or that the majority of African societies are not suited to, or ready for, democratic government? The answers to both questions are negative. The major reason for disappointment in the outcome of the successful challenge to "patrimonial autocracies" is a misunderstanding both of the conditions for democratic societies and of the time-span of the process necessary for establishing democracies. No country in the world that can be classified as democratic achieved a reasonably democratic system of governing society in the space of a few years, or even in a decade or two. Democratic government everywhere has grown by incremental stages. For example, it took Britain almost a century from the adoption of its Reform Act before women were given the right to vote; and in "democratic" Switzerland, this right has not yet been won. In the United States, it took almost two centuries to create conditions where African Americans could participate fully in the electoral process. Always and everywhere, there has been a longish transition period leading through various stages of democracy. The error made by

the Second Liberation leaders—an error which, incidentally, they were encouraged to make by the older Western
democracies—was to assume that multiparty elections on
the basis of a universal franchise would have as its outcome
a democratic government.

The conditions for achieving and maintaining democracy are, in fact, much more extensive than just holding
multi-party elections on the basis of one person, one vote.
There are at least eighteen conditions that characterize a
democratic society and which need to be fulfilled to sustain it. First and foremost is a national constitution, negotiated and accepted by representative political parties and
civic groups. Other conditions are enforceable guarantees
for human rights, for free and regular elections, and freedom of political organizations; national institutions providing for checks and balances between executive, legislative, and administrative powers; a truly independent judiciary; *habeas corpus;* freedom of movement and assembly; a
free press; academic and religious freedom; independent
trade unions; and an active civil society. Each of these takes
time to develop. Julius Nyerere once told me, when he was
reflecting on political change, that "democracy is a habit,
and habits take along time to develop." Then he added:
"Good habits can be learned slower or faster depending on
the example set by parents, or, in politics, by the leaders of
society."

It is necessary to distinguish between authentic democratic societies—which, incidentally, exist nowhere—and
those that are neither fully democratic nor authoritarian:
what can be called "transitional democracies." Those who
disagree with the idea of "transitional democracies" fail to
see the development of democracy as a slow political process involving incremental change. The stage reached in
the process can be assessed by reference to the conditions
for a democratic society listed above. Each of the principles
is usually violated at different stages in the process: elec-

THE PERIOD OF REALISM, 1988-?

60

tions aren't completely free, but are mostly loaded in favor of the incumbent governing party, and constitutions are seldom democratically negotiated, for example. Transitional arrangements should make it possible for shortcomings to be challenged at each stage of development and for improvements to be brought about incrementally. Imperialist though he was, U.S. President Theodore Roosevelt had strong democratic instincts. "I am not concerned," he said "with what theorists say about achievements for centuries ahead, only about what can be achieved tomorrow."

To sum up this section, it is possible to say that most African countries can now be classified as "transitional democracies"; five have already moved further along the road to fulfilling many of the conditions to qualify as parliamentary democracies; and a sixth, South Africa, now has a rigid constitution with justifiable rights guaranteeing all the conditions for a democratic society. The as-yet-unanswerable question is whether South Africa will become the trendsetter for the continent. In some respects, the makers of South Africa's constitution have established rights and practices that go beyond those institutionalized in even the older democracies; e.g. sex equality (the ANC's own constitutional provision is that at least one-third of its members of parliament will be women); abolition of the death penalty and flogging; and a method of appointing judges which safeguards against political appointments.

Let us turn our attention to the problems of ethnicity that caused many of the conflicts during the period of disillusionment. We all continue to struggle with the distinctions between racism, race prejudice, and ethnicity. Michael Banton of Oxford University has offered a useful definition which emphasizes that the chief difference between racial and ethnic relations is not simply that "race" depends upon physical indentifiability; the emphasis is on ethnic minorities as voluntary groupings. The social groups identified by *racial* labels are not simply categories of individuals, but groups which either had their *inclusive* bonds in the beginning, or have developed them in response to circumstances. Therefore, Blacks in the United States or Britain are racial insofar as they are categorized by whites, and ethnic insofar as they maintain their own distinctiveness. Similarly, this distinction can be applied to Afrikaners in South Africa, except that their "race" was marked off by other whites (the English), but they have maintained their own distinctiveness and most still wish to do so. Banton's definitions of race and ethnicity make it easier to analyze the changes that have begun to influence political systems in Africa. For example, getting away from the exclusiveness of race as defined by whites in South Africa, the Black Consciousness movement in South Africa, led by Robert Sobukwe and Steve Biko, has moved to an *inclusive* definition of ethnicity whereby all people of whatever "race" are classified as South Africans. The efforts in Africa to produce an all-inclusive ethnicity—the core requirement of a cohesive nation—have had uneven results. But those who believe it is impossible to achieve such cohesion should look to the example already cited—Tanzania, with its one hundred and fifty-six cultural groups spread across that vast East African country. Since Tanzania's independence more than thirty years ago, "tribalism" has played virtually no part in the country's politics, and there has been no serious conflict between the different "tribes" or cultural groups. The principal reason for this was a system that ensured equal entry into and participation in politics, and a skillfully crafted electoral system under which no candidate is allowed to use his or her tribal affiliation or religion in campaigning. There are other novel features to ensure absolute equality of opportunity between candidates in an election campaign. Tanzania's possible future problems are not ethnic but religious, arising from a conflict between groups of Muslims in Zanzibar.

A different electoral system to counter ethnic rivalries

was adopted in the very multicultural society of Nigeria before the military took over. To qualify for the right to compete in elections, political parties had to have a percentage of registered members in every one of the twenty-one states; and to win they needed to obtain 12 percent of the vote in each state. This ensured that political parties have to develop national programs with an appeal that cannot be based on only one ethnic group, region, or state.

A unique system to reduce, if not altogether eliminate, conflict between the country's major ethnic communities was adopted in Ethiopia after the overthrow of the military Marxist regime of Mengistu Haile Mariam. It flies in the face of the approach taken by the first postcolonial regimes, which denounced any mention of tribalism or race as colonialist language. The young generation of Ethiopians who triumphed in the struggle against the Mengistu regime based their approach to a new constitution for Africa's oldest independent state on an acknowledgment that race was one of the principal causes of conflict in the country's history; they therefore decided to create a federation of states based on the ethnicity of the major cultural group in each of the eight states, and to provide for culturally autonomous enclaves for the strongest minorities within each state. A federal constitution of ethnically based states is an entirely novel contribution to the problems of multicultural countries. One is tempted to speculate what the history of Yugoslavia might have been if a post-Tito constitution had followed the Ethiopian pattern. It is still too soon to make any verdict on the success of the Ethiopian model.

In many African countries, the problems presented by ethnicity have been overcome, or made more manageable, through constructing governments that are more representative of ethnic or regional communities. The change for the better in the new period of realism is that problems of ethnicity are no longer being swept under the carpet. However, a few countries remain destabilized by ethnic conflict—notably the Hutu-Tutsi conflict in Rwanda and Burundi; strife between the Arab and Black Riverine people in Mauritania; and the current conflict between two rival groups in Congo-Brazzaville. The Kalenjin–Kikuyu–Luo conflict in Kenya is typical of some other situations where a major ethnic group has been allowed to enjoy the lion's share of the benefits accruing from its hold on power.

Those who foresaw bloodshed in South Africa between white and Black communities, and between the different Black cultural groups—especially the Xhosas and Zulus—have largely been proven wrong. The peaceful transition of political (though not yet economic) power from a still strongly entrenched white minority to a Black majority is unique in modern history. It has been described as a miracle; but this invocation of a magical act detracts from the actual practical steps that went into bringing about the remarkable transformation of South Africa. It was not a miracle but hardheaded politics and economic realities that produced the conditions for successful negotiations for the handover of power. Although the country as a whole has welcomed the creation of what Archbishop Tutu described as the "birth of the Rainbow nation," a few ethnic problems remain. The defeat of the Afrikaners has not yet been absorbed by all of that strong and influential community; and a section of Zulus—mainly among the non-urbanized traditionalists who belong to Chief Buthelezi's Inkatha Party—still cling to the dream of some form of Zulu autonomy; however, the "Zulu nation" has itself become divided in its political loyalties, which illustrates the fallacy of generalizations about the homogeneity of even large and strong "tribal" communities. It is difficult to forecast the future of a society like Sudan that is deeply cleaved by culture, especially religion. Secession is an option for the South, but the North does not want to lose the oil resources that lie mainly in the South; also, several million Southerners

THE PERIOD OF REALISM, 1988–?

live in and around Khartoum in the North and, besides, the Southern ethnic communities have their own animosities. A form of federalism would seem to be the only logical solution.

Two important features of this period of realism remain to be considered: the Pan-Africanist ideals of the Organization of African Unity, and the continent's immediate economic future.

In the period of romanticism, Pan-Africanism was seen as a solution to the balkanized condition of the continent after independence. The instrument to fulfill this ambition was the Organization of African Unity (OAU). In the period of disillusionment, the OAU had little success in promoting economic unity in the continent; its three major successes have continued to be the contribution it has made to the overthrow of the remnants of colonialism in white-ruled Southern Africa; its ability to express an African voice in international forums; and its prevention of border conflicts. But it has not so far played a distinguished role in either preventing or ending violent conflicts within or between its member-states. This is ascribable to the fact that a key principle in the OAU charter prohibited it from intervening in the internal affairs of its members—a restriction that was finally overcome in 1990 when the OAU summit of heads of state unanimously agreed to establish a mechanism for the prevention and management resolution of conflicts in the continent. This represented a major shift in the willingness of Africa's leaders to take responsibility for handling conflict situations in their continent. It now remains to be seen how effectively this mechanism can be made to work in situations like those in Rwanda and Burundi.

Finally, there are the overarching issues of the continent's economic and social decline. With only a few exceptions, Africa's present leaders are broadly agreed on the direction of economic policy, and the requirements for its success. They have unanimously endorsed a program accepting that successful economic development is linked to democracy; they have accepted the need for an enlarged private sector and the shrinking of the state sector (for example, by dismantling the system of parastatals); they have come to terms with multinational corporations; and they have agreed to limit budget deficits to 3 percent per annum even though it usually involves reductions in spending on education, health, and welfare. All these policies are in line with the neo-liberal doctrine preached by the West.

Welcoming these changes, Frank Savage, chairman of Alliance Capital Management, exulted that African leaders had "gotten religion" in regard to the private sector. Irrespective of the individual merits of each of the policies in current Western "economic correctness," collectively they reflect acceptance of, or submission to, the neo-liberal economic doctrines of the Western industrial nations. They have been driven to accept, under internal and international pressure, that the price to be paid for foreign aid, possible relief from their heavy foreign debt, and attracting foreign capital investment, is to follow the West's prescription for economic growth.

So far, twenty-nine African governments have signed up for the Structural Adjustment Programs (SAPs) of the World Bank. Despite some claims of success in countries like Ghana and Mozambique, the SAP experiment has failed to promote sustainable economic growth. A World Bank Policy Research Working Paper reported in 1992 that the Bank's support for adjustment programs "has not significantly affected economic growth and has contributed to a statistically significant drop in investment ratio. . . ." Further, gross domestic savings as a percentage of the GDP fell in fourteen of the twenty-nine countries signed up for SAP and were as low as about 8 percent, compared with 22 percent for non-SAP countries. There were also other negative findings.

THE PERIOD OF REALISM, 1988–?

Not only did World Bank policies not help most countries, but they actually harmed and distorted local economic development, for example, by demanding cutbacks in the national budgets of Zimbabwe, Zambia, Namibia, Kenya, and other countries, which led to a substantial reduction in the sums spent on education—although it is essential to produce an educated and trained labor force—and on health, which simply shifted present spending on the health service to greater spending in the future because of predictable declines in health conditions. The Bank's encouragement to grow more export crops contributed to undermining traditional local markets and food production, and increased dependency on the swings of the world market prices for commodities. An Oxfam study showed that the Bank's SAP program has added to unemployment in Africa. It concludes that "the reality of SAPs is that they have locked Africa into a downward spiral of disinvestment and low growth, all in the familiar name of defeating inflation."

The World Bank has admitted that even the average poor person in its star performer, Ghana, will not cross the poverty line for another fifty years. The World Bank's new president, James Wolfenson, has accepted what the Bank's critics have long argued: "One thing," he said, "which has been learnt in recent years is an absolute recognition that, unless you have sound social policies, you cannot have sound economic policies. That is crystal clear. Unless you have a solid base with the people, unless you are concerned with the rights of the individual, unless you are concerned with elements of social responsibility and social justice, you cannot have peace and you cannot have safe investing." How does he square this obvious truth with the insistence of the World Bank and IMF that expenditures on such social programs as health and education be cut?

While Africa now waits to see how Wolfenson's different approach is going to manifest itself in World Bank policies, an even greater threat to Africa's economic future

threatens the hopes fostered during the period of realism—
it is called globalization, the new ideology for restructuring global politics and economics, which the International
Forum on Globalization says "may prove as historically significant as any event since the Industrial Revolution." Whatever the advantages globalization holds for the rich industrial world, what is clear is that it will serve to tie the
economics of developing countries to the chariot wheels of
the Big Seven's juggernaut, and that it will take little
account of the conditions needed to revitalize local economies. The International Forum of Globalization, which was
initiated in the United States by sixty economists, schol-
ars, and writers and now has forty supporting organizations in eighteen countries, argues that globalization will
reinforce the expansion of "economic colonization of the
South by the North; that it will widen the gaps between
rich and poor countries; and that it will produce a sharp
increase in unemployment in both the North and the
South." Whether this dark scenario is a correct presentation
of the effects of globalization, the reality is that Africa, in
common with developing countries in other continents, is
being faced with the alternative of refusing to open its
economies to the demands of globalization or being left to
battle on its own on the margins of the new economic revolution.

Africa's Period of Realism has coincided with wrench-
ing changes in the world economy. Having been launched
into independence at the beginning of the end of the age
of imperialism, Africa now faces the problems of post-
imperialism and globalization. As defined by Richard Sklar,
post-imperialism signifies the evolution of world politics
from imperial systems of power to the emergence of a global society.[20] He and others envision the possible growth of
what they describe as a "corporate international bourgeoisie" —
the principal source of bourgeois dynamism in the global
advance toward a post-imperial age. Is Africa at the begin-

ning of a new period of imperialism, based not on territorial occupation but on control of the world's resources through the movement of capital? As Robert Reich has pointed out, since "every modern national economy is a region of the global economy," none can completely escape from the net of globalization.[21] What will be the ultimate effects of the domination of the world economy by the eight most powerful economic nations and the leading 520 multinationals (151 US-based and 149 Japan-based) which, by 1982, already accounted for one-third of the total world output?

Although globalization is acknowledged to have contributed to raising living standards and foreign investors have, so far, poured one trillion dollars into developing economies in the 1990s, its record to date is dangerously uneven. According to Peter Sutherland, a director of Goldman Sachs International, chairman of British Petroleum, and chairman of the New York–based Overseas Development Council:

> While globalization has raised living standards for many, it has made life more difficult for those dislocated by change and it threatens to leave part of the world behind. It is no coincidence that the disappointing economic performance in much of Sub-Saharan Africa reflects a failure to integrate into the world economy and, thus, trade successfully and attract investment. . . . *There is no doubt that globalization has in some way weakened the independence of national governments and made life less predictable for many individuals.* But those who would erect barriers to trade and investment to try to recapture an earlier era of independence confuse the cause and effect of globalization. In pursuit of higher living standards, we have created this new world of global markets and instant communication to deliver gains in efficiency and competition that are beyond the powers of national governments.[22]

Not everybody will agree with Sutherland's challenging conclusion—certainly not Adebayo Adedeji, former UN Under-Secretary General, Executive Secretary of the Economic Commission for Africa (1975–1991), and now Executive Director of the African Center for Development and Strategic Studies. He writes:

> Africa will only be able to invent a future for itself that will bring rising prospects of prosperity through total commitment to its own programs and through their vigorous implementation. The politics of economic policy consist not only in their conceptualization, articulation, adoption and popularization, but also in total and unrelenting commitment to implementation. It is only by so doing that Africa, particularly sub-Saharan Africa, can rediscover its self-respect and remold its image.[23]

Finally, I am left with the crucial question whether globalization involves just the "transfer of power" by national governments to forces controlling international finance and markets; or does globalization in fact involve an actual "shift in power"? Alvin Toffler's conceptual theory about the difference between "transfer of power" and "power-shift" strikes me as crucially important in studying the process of decolonization and the dramatic change in South Africa. Toffler's distinction between the two is that "power shift" involves a deep-level change in the very nature of power that transforms power—a restructuring of the total system.[24] Those who support the theory of "power shifts" suggest they have, in fact, occurred only seldom in history: for example, the spread of Christianity (350–550), the spread of the Roman Empire (ninth century), the rise of federalism (ninth–fourteenth centuries), the Renaissance (1350–1550), the rise of the centralized nation-state (1500–1700), the rise of commercial capitalism, the Enlightenment (1770–1820), the French Revolution, and the Industrial Revolution (eighteenth century). Did decolonization, in fact, represent only a transfer of power by the Western powers, but not a power-shift between Africa and the West, and between what we now call the Third World and the powerful industrial nations?

THE PERIOD OF REALISM, 1988–?

In South Africa, we have seen the transfer of political but not of economic power, so there has not yet been a power-shift. But the large question is whether globalization represents the beginning of a power-shift that will completely redefine the economic relations between the developed and the developing nations, and what freedom and independent power the latter possess to oppose or withstand globalization, or select what is useful to them. The continent's future may well depend on what stand its leaders, and those supporting globalization, take.

FOUR

A Period of Renaissance?

As we speak of an African renaissance, we project into both the
past and the future. I speak here of the emergence of Homo
sapiens on the African continent, of African works of art in
South Africa that are over a thousand years old.
I speak of the continuum in the fine arts that encompasses the varied artistic creations of the Nubians and the Egyptians, the
Benin bronzes of Nigeria and the intricate sculptures of the
Makonde of Tanzania and Mozambique. I speak of the
centuries-old contributions to the evolution of religious thought
made by the Christians of Ethiopia and the Muslims of Nigeria.
When I survey all this and much more besides, I find nothing to
sustain the long-held dogma of African exceptionalism, according
to which the colour black becomes a symbol of fear, evil and death.
—South Africa's vice-president, Thabo Mbeki,
Business Day, Johannesburg, 14 April 1998.

Before leaving your country to return to my native Ghana, I
would like to pen some warnings about the enthusiasm I
have noted here about your deputy president's promotion of
what he calls the "African renaissance."
The word "renaissance" presupposes a "naissance" (i.e., a "birth"
in French) before there can be a "rebirth" or renaissance. As an
African I love my continent but, as a professor of history, it is
hard for me to agree that we have ever had our "naissance" or
"birth." I think Mbeki should speak of an African birth now
becoming possible but only because, at the bottom end of the
twentieth century, we Africans have begun at last to realise
the importance of the impact of European culture, science, language
and liberty upon our ways. Our birth has still to come, let alone our

rebirth.I believe, as did Kwame Nkrumah, that "when colonial-
ism is placed on the scales, it will tip them in our favour." I hope
you will publish this warning so that your readers do not become
over-expectant of our new euphoria in our continent.
—Professor Wycliff Ogupu.
Sunday Times, *Johannesburg,* 22 May 1998.

At the end of the century, the mood of the continent has come full cycle, repeating the euphoria at its beginning — a joyful optimism about the dawn of an African renaissance, but this time around there is the sobering experience of four decades of difficulties in confronting the complex problems inherent in the creation of new independent states, and of the obstacles in the way of establishing continental unity, which remains an unfulfilled but still undimmed dream. Also, as before, there are the skeptical voices with messages reminiscent of the doubts expressed by the Ivorian leader Felix Houphouet-Boigny in the late 1950s.

There is also another difference: the absence this time of prophetic voices and continental role models like Kwame Nkrumah, Sékou Touré, Jomo Kenyatta, Tom Mboya, Julius Nyerere, Gamal Nasser, Amilcar Cabral, Ben Bella, and Patrice Lumumba; and stalwart conservatives like Houphouet-Boigny, the Liberian Tubman, the Tunisian Habib Bourguiba, and the historic figure of Haile Selassie. At the century's end, only one African name resonates throughout the continent — Nelson Mandela, already in his declining years. His dauphin, Thabo Mbeki, has yet to establish his credentials as a continental spokesman for the new renaissance.

FUTURE OF THE NATION-STATE

Whatever other illusions and institutions were shattered by the disorder and turmoil that characterized the formative period of Africa's nation-states, one idea has endured: the need for and importance of a sovereign nation-state. The only debate around this concept has been a relatively insubstantial questioning of the idea of a *centralized* nation-state, principally by proponents of federalism. But only in the continent's most populous country, Nigeria, did the federalists win, while an unique experiment of an ethnic federal state has begun to take shape in Ethiopia. The Cameroons, which began independence as a semi-federalist state, soon lost this character. The Senegal-Mali and Sene-gambia "confederations" crumbled rapidly, as did the union of Cape Verde and Guinea-Bissau. The *Majimbo* demand of a collection of the Kalenjin communities in Kenya was rejected even before independence. The Tanzania Repub-lic's duality between the mainland Tanganyika and the islands of Zanzibar and Pemba was never an altogether happy partnership. While the democratic South African constitution allows for a rudimentary federal structure through its nine provinces, the demand by a sizeable minority of Afrikaners for a distinctive state of their own within the Union cannot yet be written off as a lost cause. Federalism, however, became an "f-word" for the early generation of African nationalists who saw it as an attempt to weaken the postcolonial centralized state.

Only three serious attempts were made to set up break-away independent states. The most serious was the Ibo struggle to create the secessionist Biafra republic, which plunged Nigeria into a civil war. The second was Moise Tshombe's bid, with the support of his foreign allies (Bel-gium, Rhodesia, and a number of powerful financial inter-ests), to bring about Katanga's secession from Zaire. (A common factor of both these secessionist movements is their mineral wealth—oil in Iboland and the "geological scandal" of minerals in Katanga.) The third secessionist challenge was made in Somalia during the bitter clan struggles for power after the overthrow of Siad Barre's military regime. At the time of writing, the future of the former British protectorate, the Republic of Somaliland, was still problematic. Eritrea's break away from Ethiopia was sui generis; it tore up the system imposed on the territory by Emperor Haile Selassie and re-established the country's earlier status separate from Ethiopia.

In sum, although Africa came to its independence as a balkanized continent of fifty-five states—far more than on any other continent—the reality of sovereign statehood has remained unchallenged, except by persistent right-wing lobbies in Europe and the United States—supported even by some prominent Africanist academics—who argue that the "failure" of many of the nation states in Sub-Saharan Africa is due to the unpreparedness and lack of experience of Africans to run a modern state. Their preferred "solution" is for the United Nations to establish a temporary trusteeship over "collapsed" states. Even in the unlikely instance that some African states might voluntarily relinquish their sovereignty, even temporarily, one wonders what group of UN members would be prepared to undertake a recolonizing role?

The implicit racism underlying this unrealistic proposal harks back to the arguments deployed by the opponents of decolonization in the 1940s and 1950s that Africans either were not "ready" for independence or were fundamentally incapable of ruling themselves. Such arguments, familiar to the anti-colonial movements, were succinctly countered by the Black American educationist James Aggrey, who said that the only way to learn to play the violin was to practice on it. This was the theme of the seminal book *Attitude to Africa*, produced by the Rev. Michael Scott's Africa Bureau. [25] It was also the argument deployed by the distinguished novelist and former Nigerian colonial servant Joyce Carey in *The Case for African Freedom*. Now the practice is over, and the task for the future is to restore the fortunes of the state by creating relevant, viable, and sustainable institutions to ensure their ability to withstand coups and the manipulations of powerful pressure groups, to maintain lawful order, to minimize corruption, and to promote economic growth and development. This is a tall order.

A serious approach to a fresh start in Africa requires, among other reforms, a willingness to reconsider the nature of the state, especially in countries fractured by seemingly irreconcilable ethnic, regional, and religious conflicts, such as those in Rwanda, Burundi, and Sudan, and potentially also in Algeria, where, if the intra-Muslim conflict deepens, the Berbers (like the Southern Sudanese) are most unlikely to accept the conditions of a fundamentalist Islamic Republic.

There are few parallels between the European Renaissance and a potential African Renaissance: the former was culturally driven, initially inspired by the exiled Roman painter Giotto; the latter is driven, as yet, less by a revitalization of culture than by modernizing social, political, and economic forces engaged in a radical questioning of tradition, the structuring of the post-colonial capitalist international state, and the relationship between Africa and a westernized international society. While the European Renaissance spanned a century before reaching its full flowering, an African Renaissance could progress more rapidly in the modern world of science, high technology, information systems, and international interdependency.

Stripped of romanticism, the challenges that need to be confronted if there is to be a genuine African Renaissance are: weak and vulnerable states with regimes unable to maintain lawful order and to promote equitable economic development; ethnic conflicts; population and urban explosions; continuous decline of traditional rural life and a system of agriculture balanced between the production of food for local needs and for export cash crops; religious fundamentalism; desertification and environmental degradation; stultifying economics; inadequate health services to cope with HIV/AIDS, tuberculosis, and other pandemics; poverty and unemployment; and globalization.

While a strongly centralized state is probably justified to deal with the problems of the security and divisiveness inherent in newly independent, fragile, nascent states, experience has shown that such a state often lacks the flexibility to peacefully accommodate the conflicting interests of multicultural or multinational societies, and that the security forces needed to maintain a centralized state often end up as a threat to the state itself through coups and other actions.

The centralized unitary state has been substantially transformed in Europe, the Americas, and the Indian subcontinent, and is still undergoing changes to relieve pressures by, for example, redistributing power from the center to peripheral states, provinces, or regions, with greater or lesser characteristics of federalism—ranging from the constitutions of the United States and India to those of Australia, Canada, and Germany. This approach has ensured periods of reasonable stability based on a manageable state of tension between the center and the periphery. But, in time, as the peripheral "statelets" have grown economically and local patriotism has taken root, pressures have gradually forced a greater devolution of power as exemplified by the autonomy granted to Scotland and Wales within the framework of Great Britain. It would be surprising if, during the coming century, similar constitutional reforms providing for the devolution of power were not to occur in Africa as confidence grows in the integrity of the state.

Federalism comes in many forms and is of course not a

solution for all ethnic, religious, and other types of conflict; but it is less rigid and procrustean than the centralized unitary state, still the dominant form of government in Africa.

A federal system in Nigeria, which evolved progressively from three states at independence to twenty-six, has successfully held a multinational country together through a bitter civil war and a series of disastrous military regimes.

The military remains the most immediately serious challenge to the continent's political stability. It will continue to remain the destabilizing factor so long as a relatively small handful of soldiers can hold the state for ransom. Since it will take time before democratic institutions, an effective civil society, and a system of counterbalancing security forces can be established to deter coupists, the first test of a new generation of African leaders will therefore be to implement a strategy to deter parvenu military men like the deplorable Amins, Bokassas, Abachas, Does, Mengistu Haile Mariams, el-Bashiers, and even the less disreputable but still discreditable Musevenis and Rawlings, from short-circuiting the democratic process. The elements of such a strategy are at hand, and have often been spoken about, but never implemented. They include such measures as an enforceable threat to punish coupist leaders in the same way as are other categories of "war criminals." Instead of treating them as heads of state even while they grossly abuse their power and, if they survive long enough, granting them either *de facto* or even *de jure* recognition, they should be isolated and treated as pariahs. OAU member states should be bound by treaty not to recognize the legitimacy of any regime produced by a coup. This should be backed by a parallel commitment of the UN, the European Union, the two Commonwealths (former British and former USSR), and the non-aligned states to follow suit; and by a convention binding international financial institutions and trade organizations to refuse loans to and to suspend trade relations with illegitimate regimes. From the start of a coup, the OAU should implement its statutes to provide an intervention force if negotiations fail to end the coup.

If all of this sounds a bit far-fetched, it should be pointed out that the essential elements of each of these proposals has already been accepted, in principle, by either the OAU or other international bodies, and action along these lines was taken in Sierra Leone. The weakness in the past has been that the measures have been implemented mostly unilaterally, selectively, and tardily. The ground should already now be prepared to negotiate a strategy to outlaw coups along the lines set out above. This would demonstrate a seriousness of purpose to give democracy a chance to flower.

PROSPECTS FOR A POLITICAL RENAISSANCE

All but a half a dozen of the continent's fifty-six states can already be classified as transitional democracies; that is, they provide for some of the prerequisites for democratic government, such as a plural political system and the right of political parties to engage in regularly held free elections for a national parliament. But these measures do not by themselves guarantee political freedom. (For a full list of the principles governing a democratic society, see the previous chapter.) The most comprehensive democratic constitution in the continent is the one negotiated in the "new" South Africa. It could become the model for the rest of the continent.

The emergence of a non-racial democratic South Africa from the ruins of apartheid is seen by many as the beginning of an African Renaissance. Whether South Africa will indeed become a beacon for the rest of the continent will depend largely on developments in the country over the five-to-seven-year period after the retirement of President Mandela. After more than three centuries of one of the most damaging racist political systems in modern times, South Africa is not yet a normal society. While the transition period presided over by Mandela was surprisingly peaceful and promising, the period of transformation away from what is still a white-privileging society is bound to be more difficult and controversial. The fallout of a serious conflict in the south could almost certainly affect developments in the north.

PROSPECTS FOR AN ECONOMIC AND SOCIAL RENAISSANCE IN A GLOBALIZED WORLD

After decades of economic decline, it is understandable if people are skeptical about a dramatic economic recovery. But the signs of recovery are already unmistakable. To put the situation in perspective, it is necessary to present the negative picture first. The mere recital of statistics can produce two different responses: one is to evoke emotions of sympathy, charity, and guilt; the other is a reminder of the cost of hospitals, medicines, urban and rural development programs, employment schemes, the provision of fresh water, and the protection of the environment. Some of the following figures have been quoted before, but they need repeating in a different context to be able to gauge more accurately what is involved to achieve significant changes in the human and natural environment.

About 45 percent of the approximately 590 million people in Sub-Saharan Africa (1997 estimate) live below the poverty line, implying that their potential human resources are undeveloped and underutilized, while their needs keep growing. Life expectancy in Africa is 51 years, compared to 59 in South Asia and 68 in Latin America. One-quarter of Africans in some regions suffer from HIV/AIDS. Caring for all of them in hospitals or hospices would absorb all the funds now allocated to the sub-continent's total health budgets. WHO's figures show that the health of mothers and children in Africa is the worst in the world. Since 1983, infant mortality has soared from 3 to 9 percent in certain regions; some 4.2 million neo-natal deaths occur every year, of which 3 million occur in the first week following birth. A further WHO study shows that drinking water and sanitation in Sub-Saharan Africa (SSA) are "the most deplorable on earth."[26] More than half of the region's people lack safe drinking water; and 344 million lack adequate sewerage. The incidence of poverty in SSA is expected to stay at the 1985 level in the year 2000, with an increase of more than 45 percent in the number of those living in poverty. With an annual average growth rate of approximately 2 percent, Africa's population is expected to double to 1.2 billion by 2030, intensifying the problems listed above.

According to a World Bank Task Force in December 1996, economic growth rates of at least 6.5 percent are needed if typical SSA countries are to reduce poverty. What are the chances of Africa staging an economic recovery to at least 6.5 percent? By mid-1998, this target was already within the grasp of most countries, encouraging the World Bank to predict a modest growth rate of 7 percent by the year 2000. Others forecast a 10 percent growth rate in some countries. In 1997, the Economic Intelligence Unit reckoned that five out of twenty of the world's fastest-growing economies were in Africa. There will be winners and losers, and Africa, like all other continents and economies, is likely to develop unevenly. While economic growth is important, the question that needs to be asked is who will benefit from this greater national wealth. (Despite the much vaunted growth of the Asian Tigers, at the height of their success there were one billion people living in poverty in their region.) The answer is that it depends on whether accountable democratic governments develop simultaneously with economic growth.

The prospect of an African Renaissance comes at a time when the international community stands on the brink of a historic power-shift[27] — not just a change in economic power relations but a seismic change in world economic power. The historical movement called globalization has developed a momentum that is already inexorable. It coincides with a new Information Age defined by Manual Casrills[28] as "the network society," which will increasingly dominate the production of wealth and spread its tentacles into more and more crevices of people's lives. It will have three main consequences: an information technology which allows a burgeoning number of transactions to take place globally and simultaneously; cultural and social movements which radically question tradition; the restructuring of capitalism and the state which began to take place in the 1980s, and which freed capital from restraint to move freely across the globe. Commenting on the work of Casrills and a small group of sociologists like Anthony Giddens, Alain Touraine, and Ulrich Beck, John Lloyd wrote:

> We are at the start of something new and something big. For the first time the world is organized by a common set of capitalist rules—and not just capitalism but informational capitalism, or internationalism, which means that money is made from applying knowledge to processes and continually upgrading and refining both the knowledge and the process. Everything is subordinated to the requirements of this revolutionary system, including capitalism and the capitalists themselves.[29]

Expanding on this theme, John Gray, professor of politics of Oxford University, has this to say: "The spread of new technologies throughout the world is not working to advance human freedom. Instead it has resulted in the emancipation of market forces from social and political control. By allowing that freedom to world markets we ensure that the age of globalization will be remembered as another turn in the history of servitude."[30] Adding his voice to the dangers inherent in globalization, the world's leading financier and profiteer from the present system, George Soros, warned: "The present situation is comparable to that at the turn of the past century. It was the golden age of capitalism, characterized by the principle laissez-faire, so is the present. The earlier period was in some ways more stable."[31] Elsewhere, Soros explained: "I am afraid that the prevailing view, which is one of extending the market mechanism to all domains, has the potential of destroying society. Unless we review our concepts of markets, our understanding of markets, they will collapse because we are creating global markets, global financial markets, without understanding their true nature. . . . With the accumulation of wealth there comes increasing social division and *the majority of people don't benefit from the global economy*, even though we are all getting richer as countries and as a globe—there are also tremendous benefits from technological advance and so on. So there are a lot of good things going on, but also a lot of bad things. We have to deal with the bad things"[32] (my italics). Soros believes that "because socialism is dead," the only alternative is nationalism.

The debate about globalization, the Information Age, and technology is crucial to the future, not only of the economics of Third World countries, but also limitation on their political independence. Africa is already globalized, according to Paul Collier,[33] head of the World Bank's research department, but in the wrong way: "Its trade has become more concentrated in primary products, and its integration into the global capital markets has been the result. *An estimated 70 percent of Africa's private wealth is being invested outside the continent.* Although globalization is inescapable—and holds some advantage—it need not encompass all the demands of what is being described as 'enlightenment capitalism.'" The advice given to African participants in an IMF seminar by its managing director, Michael Camdessus, was: "You need to prepare your own strategy that would enable Africa to maximize the benefits of globalization while avoiding its perils."[34] The success of a struggle to limit the impact of what is certain to be seen as the threat of "a new round of neo-colonialism," is bound to determine the progress and direction of Africa's economic recovery.

Population and Urban Explosion

Thirty years after the turn of the millennium, Africa's population is projected to reach around 1.2 billion, having more than doubled in a single generation. Notwithstanding the speed with which the "empty spaces" in the continent are filling up, there has been a significant lack of discussion about the impact of the population explosion on the continent's economy and social environment. The Muslim societies which stretch from North Nigeria to the Maghrib countries in the north, and the Roman Catholic confessors of countries like Kenya, firmly oppose family planning and abortion as a matter of religious principle and are unlikely to be swayed from their position, at least for the foreseeable future. Even countries which encourage family planning—like South Africa, Zimbabwe, and Uganda—accord a low priority to action designed to curb the population explosion, probably for traditional reasons and because, as yet, no real pressure has been felt on the land except in a few countries like Rwanda, Burundi, Lesotho, and, more recently, Kenya. Around 80 percent of Africans were still living in rural areas toward the end of the twentieth century. They regard large families as necessary to augment their domestic labor force; as insurance against the depletion of family size through high rates of infant mortality; and for the bride price (lobola) that comes with the marriage of girls. A clash between tradition-bound Africa and its modernizing societies over population growth is inevitable, and is likely to claim a higher priority in the future for three reasons: its absorption of economic and social resources, such as education and health; its seriously deleterious effects on urban societies; and the growing consciousness of women who refuse to have their lives circumscribed by a continuous two- to three-year cycle of childbearing.

The actual impact of population growth on economic development remains a subject of controversy among economists, but they increasingly come to support the findings of a 1990 World Bank report that "the evidence points overwhelmingly to the conclusion that population growth can make an important contribution to (social advance)"; however, while "population growth can be accommodated up to a point . . . the goal of development extends beyond accommodation of an ever larger population: it is to improve people's lives."[35]

Although the developing world as a whole made economic progress in the last quarter of the twentieth century, the number of people living in "absolute poverty"—a description coined by Robert McNamara when he was president of the World Bank—increased to more than one billion, of whom 185 million lived in Sub-Saharan Africa. McNamara's definition of the "absolute poor" are those living, literally, on the margin of life. Their lives are so characterized by malnutrition, illiteracy, and disease as to be beneath any reasonable definition of human beings.[36] Those who have seen "the absolute poor" swarming in homeless family groups in India will instantly recognize this condition; up to the mid-twentieth century these conditions were comparatively rare in most of Africa, but this is no longer true. The pace of urban growth in Africa is presently the highest in the world. Whereas in 1970 only about 16 percent of the continent's population lived in urban areas, a UN study projects growth to 20 percent by the year 2000. The urban explosion and the flight from an impoverished countryside has begun to produce conditions of absolute misery in squatters' camps and slums across the continent.

Cities in the Third World are growing at a yearly rate of

3.6 percent, and at rates greater than that in some cities in Africa. Lagos in Nigeria is among the twenty-one megalopolises—mostly unplanned cities of more than ten million inhabitants—in the Third World. Nairobi, the capital of Kenya, expanded by 600 percent between 1950 and 1979. In the last decade of the apartheid years, eight million Black South Africans moved into shack towns (euphemistically called "informal settlements"). The long-drawn-out war in Sudan drove millions of people out of their homes. Almost a million in search of safety were driven into shantytowns in the sand desert around Khartoum and other northern cities. On the fringes of the Sahara, drought drove thousands of nomads on an "uncontrollable stampede" into shantytowns around Rosso in Mauritania. Lacking employment, schooling, and all the services of normal urban societies, crime flourished, rape increased exponentially, and the social fabric of family and social life disintegrated. Insecurity ruled the lives of the new immigrants to urban society.

While conditions in these exploding informal settlements are mostly appalling, they are not all necessarily a burden on the older established urban societies. Bert Hoselitz, a well-known social historian, developed the idea of "generative" and "parasitic" cities. The former are capable of maintaining a degree of sustainability and of raising the capacity of their host ecosystems, usually by means of innovative, symbiotic relations. The latter are more likely to live at the expense of their host systems to the degree of overexploiting them.

When will the exodus from the countryside to the usually harsh conditions of expanding cities end? According to estimates, the first southern continent to reach a saturation level of urbanization will be Latin America, where by about 2020, some 80 percent of the population will live in urban areas, and a further rural exodus will be small in absolute numbers. Compared with Latin America and South Asia,

Africa's urban growth will still be small in 2020 because its starting point was so low; but it is predicted to increase rapidly in the first quarter of the new millennium and to begin to overtake the population growth of Latin America.[37]

Just how these changes in the urban-rural balance are likely to influence social and economic development is unpredictable. For example, the modern assumption of a one-way migration from farms to cities is proving wrong in the Kwazulu-Natal province of South Africa and could, for similar reasons, also prove wrong in other countries with industrialized cities. A Rural Urban Studies Program of the University of Natal has come up with this finding:

> Rural to urban migration is usually assumed to be the main migration flow, and most of that has been thought to be circulatory—from rural to urban and back again, according to the rhythm of labour migration. These patterns do not seem to hold true any longer. Instead, the rural space economy is bending into a new shape as urban unemployment continues to rise. Population movement no longer seems to follow the routes pioneered by urban labour migration. For the rural poor, most population flow today is rural to rural, as the urban sector separates and breaks away into a demographic sector on its own. This surge responds to economic realities. For individuals and families facing high unemployment in a changing space economy, migration from one place to another is probably the most important economic option. By leaving a disadvantaged community of origin and moving to a better location, rural households can succeed in shifting all their constraints at once. However, under current conditions of heavy crowding in rural source communities, moving from one area to another usually means trying to improve access to wage income at the cost of losing access to land, to the production economy, and to natural resources. Migration is not an easy choice to make, and many fail and choices have changed. Unemployment in the metro shack areas has risen to record rates, forcing a fundamental change. For the first time in

history, it looks as if people can now do better in smaller rural centers than in the city. Results suggest that income levels available around the outlying cities and small towns may be rising beyond what people can get in the metropolitan shack settlements, in a thin and competitive job market, swamped with aspiring rural work-seekers.[38]

Another unpredictable factor is the possibility of population movements inside the continent. The total net flow of internal emigration over the period 1980–2010 is projected at 42 million, or 4.4 percent of the total population at the end of that period. The countries expected to receive the most internal immigrants are South Africa, Zaire, Côte d'Ivoire, and Cameroon.

A study produced for the EU Commission and the *Caisse des Dèpôts et Consignations* (France) in 1984 concluded:

> These demographic and migratory prospects highlight the fact that the problem of demographic growth and its geographical spread is the central issue in the development of Sub-Saharan Africa. A tenfold increase in the total population—and of average densities, therefore—in less than one hundred years means a complete upheaval in the use of space, in human infrastructure, in trade, in relations between man and the environment, in social structures and so on. It is by far the most significant event in African history over this period of one hundred years, the foundation in which everything must be built and designed and the imperative before which all other realities—economic and financial realities included—have to bow.

The Crisis of Unemployment

The specter of unemployment stalks the continent—as, indeed, it does most continents. Even in industrialized societies, the time when waged employment for more than 90 percent of the labor force seemed possible has passed. In Africa the rate of unemployment in the modern sector has never been much lower than 60 percent in the richer countries; in the poorer countries the jobless rate is at least 90 percent. In 1993, Tanzania's Minister of Labour and Youth Development, Hassan Diria, told his National Assembly that by 1988 only 171,000 young entrants to the labor market out of over five million were able to find jobs in the formal sector.

Even an average 10 percent growth in the economy of African countries is unlikely to make a difference of more than 15–20 percent in the number of new jobs in the formal sector, but with millions of better-educated people coming on to the labor market every year, there is no earthly hope of the employment crisis being lowered in the future except, possibly, through innovative economic reforms which would concentrate more resources on the informal than the formal sector. Growing armies of jobless youths across the continent present a challenge for which no solution is yet in prospect.

CLIMATIC CONDITIONS AND THE ENVIRONMENT

African climatic conditions are inhospitable to human society and adverse to agriculture in large parts of the continent. Four-year cycles of drought followed by torrential floods are normal in much of East and Southern Africa; swarms of locusts can devastate a year's crops in a day; malaria, a variety of fevers, trachoma, AIDS, and bilharzia reduce the physical ability of young and old to work as continuously and energetically as people in northern temperate zones.

Environmental despoliation, especially of the overworked soil and forests—though not as serious as in the United States, Russia, India, or China—is nevertheless a major cause for concern. However, pessimistic reports about deforestation in West Africa have been proven incorrect. According to studies made in West Africa, the loss of forest cover in the last years was around only a third of official estimates.[39]

Among the findings are:

- Forest loss has been systematically exaggerated in each country in West Africa—in total it is around 10 million hectares, not the usually cited 28 million. This discrepancy is a result of earlier reports vastly overestimating the area where forest "used to exist," and by considering forest lost in earlier centuries to have been lost recently.

- Forest cover in 1900 may have been more than that in 1700, following depopulation associated with slavery and colonial wars in Liberia, Ghana, and Côte d'Ivoire.

- The area capable of supporting forest has increased in recent centuries due to climatic improvement, but has varied up and down during deep climatic changes in historical times.

- Many of today's forests cover areas which were previously savanna, and may exist because of people, not despite them. The vegetation forms supposed to be the least disturbed or most "natural," are in fact the most disturbed, testifying to the capacity of people to enrich soils and vegetation.

One of the most difficult challenges remains the abatement of desertification as the Sahara, the Namib, and Kalahari deserts extend themselves virtually unarrested. The Sahel—a region stretching along the southern edge of the Sahara desert—is a harsh and fragile environment, rich in history, arts, social tradition, and environmental knowledge. Its 60 million inhabitants rank among the world's very poorest. SOS Sahel, a British-based non-governmental organization,[40] has succeeded in growing almost 32,000 seedlings, establishing 16 kilometers of shelterbeds, and training locals in relevant skills, and has recovered 1,200 acres of damaged land in Mali. But its director, Duncan Fulton, warns that there is also a cost since marginal lands brought into cultivation raise the dangers of soil exhaustion, of spreading the desert, and heightening tensions between farmers and herders. In the Northern Sudan, sand dunes currently move at a rate of nine meters every year, engulfing houses and schools and laying waste to valuable assets. Entire villages are often forced to emigrate and leave their livelihoods behind. The last prolonged drought in the 1980s virtually destroyed centuries-old nomadic communities which were forced to abandon their traditional ways of life and to establish themselves precariously on the fringes of Sahelian towns. One consequence of this development has been periodic fighting between newly settled nomadic communities and their governments over border delineations and discrimination.

ETHNICITY AND RELIGIOUS FUNDAMENTALISM

A popular tendency, especially in the west, is to attribute all conflicts in Africa to "tribalism"—a superficial, one-word explanation that also confirms the racist view of the continent as a society of pre-modern warring tribal peoples. While ethnic tensions have prevailed, to a greater or lesser extent, in many pre- and postcolonial societies, they seldom spilled over into ethnic violence. The difference is important. An informed analysis of the continent's "hot wars" since independence shows that only six could be described as inter-ethnic conflicts.

By far the worst were the genocidal conflicts between Hutus and Tutsis in Rwanda and Burundi. The Biafra war in Nigeria had ethnic origins in that the northern Hausa Fulanis reacted against the commercial success of energetic Ibo entrepreneurs. The brief military campaign in Mashonaland marked the climax of the power struggle in Zimbabwe between the Ndebeli, the principal supporters of the

Zimbabwe African National Union, and the Shona, the principal supporters of the Zimbabwe African National Union. A short-lived conflict over power in Congo-Brazzaville was between regional and ethinic groups. The war in Angola had both ethnic and international elements—ethnic in that Jonas Savimbi based his Unita Army's support on the Ovimbundu, and international because the struggle was intensified as part of the Cold War through the intervention of South Africa and the United States on the side of Unita, and the USSR and Cuba on the side of the MPLA.

What of the rest? The war in Ethiopia was fought by multiethnic forces to overthrow the military Marxist regime of Mengistu Haile Mariam. The twenty-eight-year struggle in Eritrea was fought to re-establish the country's earlier status as a separate country from Ethiopia; its roots were national rather than ethnic. The civil war in Liberia was a straightforward power struggle against a discredited military regime. So was the shorter conflict in Sierra Leone. The post-independence conflict in Zaire began as a struggle for the unity of the country when Moise Tshombe, aided and abetted by powerful Belgian and other mining interests, tried to bring about Katanga's secession after the abrupt ending of Belgium's colonial rule. The conflict in Mozambique began as a liberation struggle against Portuguese colonialism but later changed its character when Ian Smith's Rhodesian regime and, later, South Africa intervened to promote their own interests by creating and sustaining a rebel movement, Renamo. The longest war in the continent, the one in Sudan, was fought about two issues—opposition to Islamic fundamentalism and support for a democratic constitution.

Two aspects of ethnicity in Africa deserve special attention. The first is the speed with which reconciliation occurs at the end of a conflict. It began, for example, within days after the end of the bitter Biafra War, when the defeated Ibo military leaders were welcomed into the federal officers'

92

messes for beer and convivial talk about their different roles in the war; there was no talk of revenge and, within months, Ibos were being absorbed into the federal political system and the economy. Perhaps the outstanding example of the capacity of Africans for non-vengeful reconciliation was what happened in South Africa after the collapse of the apartheid system—an accomplishment which stands in sharp contrast with what happened after the American Civil War.

The second, crucially important, aspect of ethnicity in Africa is the feasibility of diminishing tribal politics and rivalries through appropriate constitutional arrangements. The outstanding example has been the virtually complete absence of conflicts among the one hundred fifty-six tribes in Tanzania since independence. This success was achieved, inter alia, through an electoral system that precluded the exploitation of tribal or religious issues in campaigning for votes, and by methods to ensure free and fair elections. Other measures included a fair balance of regional representatives in the cabinet and in other government positions. The more recent conflicts between the mainland of Tanzania and the islands of Zanzibar and, especially, Pemba, are not ethnic in origin but are essentially a quarrel over alleged regional neglect, inflamed by the introduction of an Islamic religious element.

A new system of elections in Nigeria required that a successful president and political party had to secure a percentage of votes in each of the county's states, thereby ensuring national representativity while at the same time making it counterproductive to advance the interests of any one state or regime.

However, there are situations in some countries where the cultural cleavage is so wide (e.g. Mauritania and Sudan), or the fear of the change in the balance of power so strong, (e.g. the Hausa-Fulani emirate states of Nigeria), or the determination of traditional minority communities to protect their culture so great (e.g. the Berbers in Algeria and the Afrikaners in South Africa) that the possibility of ethnic-centered conflict cannot be entirely overlooked.

The rise of religious fundamentalism has been a growing phenomenon in the latter half of the twentieth century: Jewish Orthodox fundamentalism in Israel; Hindu fundamentalism in India; New Right Christian fundamentalism in the United States; and Islamic fundamentalism in a number of Muslim countries. In different degrees, all of these owe their origins and growth to similar factors: alienation from the dominant political and social systems; hostility to foreign influences; frustrations over poverty or status positions within the modern economic system; and fears about threats to the religious and cultural traditions of strong communities.

The phenomenon of religious fundamentalism began to show itself in Sub-Saharan Africa only in the 1990s, after a military regime influenced by a Muslim brotherhood came to power in Sudan in the late 1980s. Its ideological leader, Dr. Tourabi, set up a center in Khartoum, supported by the regime, for the purpose of propagating the Koran in neighboring countries, including Egypt, where a Muslim brotherhood had striven unsuccessfully for almost a century to turn the country into a fundamentalist Islamic republic. The success of the Muslim brotherhood in turning Sudan into an Islamic republic had two major results: it brought about a division between fundamentalists and the two dominant traditional Muslim sects—the Ansars and the Khatmia; and it triggered a civil war between the mainly Muslim/Arab north and the largely Christian and animist Negro south.

A different Muslim proselytizing movement, centered in Libya, was sponsored by Muammer Gadhafi. Although opposed to the fundamentalists, the Libyan leader's declared ambition is to convert Africa into an Islamic continent. Meanwhile, the fundamentalists have begun to operate

A PERIOD OF RENAISSANCE?

against Gadhafi and pose a political threat to his idiosyn-
cratic regime.

In Algeria, murderous campaigns launched in the 1990s
by Muslim fundamentalists turned the country into a
bloody battlefield. The outcome of the struggle there was
still undecided at the time of writing. Although the Muslim fundamentalists' only outright success in Africa has
been in Sudan—where its future is still uncertain—the
seeds of their ideology have been sown in the continent.
Without a renaissance in Africa, religious fundamentalism
might well become a major destabilizing factor in the next
century.

PREDICTING THE FUTURE

How will Africa look in the first half of the new century? Will the much-hyped renaissance have taken root
and contributed to producing fifty-five stable, lawful and
orderly, modernized democratic states? That is the hope,
but what are the realistic chances of this happening?

Fully cognizant of unknowable and therefore unpredictable factors, I offer three possible alternative scenarios.
First, the most hopeful. The momentum of democratization and the clamor against human rights abuses will be
maintained so that by, say, 2015, the great majority of
African states will have adopted viable democratic constitutions—either unitary, based on the South African constitution, or, preferably, federal. A modus vivendi will have
been found between the EGO-7's self-interest in gaining
control over the global economy and the interests of emergent economies in the unstoppable new era of globalization.

A second scenario is that progress toward democratization will have become stalled in a number of countries so
that the continent will end up as a piebald collection of
transitional democratic countries; and others will be ruled

by autocratic and corrupt governments rather like Central and South America before the 1950s. In this scenario, one-half to two-thirds of the continent will be "free," i.e., enjoy democratic freedoms, political stability, and sustainable economic growth; the rest will be under the rule of competing military and other autocracies and mired in corruption.

The third scenario is the worst. The democratic structures will have collapsed in South Africa (rather as in Zimbabwe in the mid-1980s); the overall economic performance of the continent will have returned to the 1960s figure below population growth, thus negative growth. Disillusionment with lack of visible success of democratic government in countries like South Africa, Botswana, and Tanzania will have led to countries embracing anti-democratic systems of government—possibly religious fundamentalist theocracies in the North, imitations of Museveni's "no party" Uganda model, or a return to military rule as in Chile under Pinochet, Nigeria, and Burma. Internal regional and ethnic conflicts will increase because of sharpened competing rivalries over a share of shrunken resources. Law and order will be at a premium; an upsurge, not only of crime, but of political violence among the urban unemployed, and of rural peasants revolts (similar to those seen recently in Mexico), will inevitably lead to increased military spending and to disregard of human rights.

Of the three proffered scenarios, the least likely is the third one, but much depends on the over-arching economic climate of the continent. If globalization in the next millennium is to usher in a new era of "capitalist imperialism"—early evidence of which is already visible—choking off economic growth in the "emerging nations," it will favor the second and perhaps even the third scenario. It could also foster virulent anti-Western attitudes as in Khomeini's Iran and parts of the Arab Middle East and Malaysia.

Most African states need to grow at least 6 percent a year in order to afford the additional cost of an average 3 percent population growth, as well as to provide minimum improvements in education, health, and social support systems and to produce internal capital for economic development. But even an average 6 percent annual growth of the economy would be inadequate without massive foreign debt relief.

As already mentioned, Africa is both blessed and cursed by its climatic and environmental conditions. Regular cycles of drought followed by periodic floods and swarms of locusts wipe out up to four years' worth of economic growth. This increases the need for even higher growth following climatic catastrophes just to catch up on the levels of previous years. Africa has no reserves to enable the surplus of "seven fat years to take care of seven lean years." As a continent, Africa has always suffered massively from endemic diseases—malarial and other mortal fevers, river blindness (trachoma), and bilharzia to mention a few.

In recent years, tuberculosis and AIDS have become the biggest killers, with the former even more widespread than the latter. The special concern about AIDS is that there is little or no basis for hope in the future. About 5,000 Africans become infected every day. Between 20 percent and 39 percent of sexually active Africans between the ages of 20 and 40 in major cities were believed in 1998 to be infected by HIV. A health specialist, James J. Zaffiro, claims that "the HIV/AIDS epidemic is crushing down on Sub-Saharan Africa more virulently and at greater human social and economic cost than anywhere else in the world." By 1993, the World Bank calculated that the annual spending in SSA for the prevention and treatment of HIV/AIDS was $90 million annually. With the exponential growth of AIDS, the burden on health budgets has already become unsustainable, exceeding the regular budgets for other hospitalized treatment and absorbing up to 50 percent of hospital beds in countries like Zaire, where the cost of treating a sick patient ranges from $132 to $1,585.

WHO projections suggest that there will be some 9 million AIDS orphans in Africa by 2000. The burden of human and financial costs of AIDS, let alone tuberculosis, will exceed the financial and material resources of most African countries by the turn of the century. Without international aid on a massive scale, there is no hope of Africa producing the resources to cope with the astronomic costs of tuberculosis and AIDS.

International aid focused on specific sectors—heath, education, training, small scale industry, and housing—will need to be increased, the burden of foreign loan indebtedness must be alleviated, and fairer trade opportunities must be provided for African exports if the first, more hopeful, scenario is to prove to be the correct one.

The only credible prediction is that by 2050 the continent's development will have produced a pattern of countries similar to Europe's or South America's at the beginning of the twentieth century. That is a range of states unequal in wealth, levels of stability, and depths of modernization. It is unlikely, but not impossible, that there will be Switzerlands; but more likely that, based on oil, there could be Venezuelas (e.g. Algeria), Brazils (South Africa and Nigeria), small but rich Gulf States (post-Gadhafi Libya) and Irans (Algeria or Egypt); medium-sized, more-or-less liberal states (Tunisia, Senegal, post-Museveini Uganda, and Morocco); and structurally impoverished and non-viable states (Rwanda, Burundi, Chad, Guinea-Bissau).

However, while these broad classifications might be roughly correct, the cited examples of countries could be different. The difficulty about predicting the future of "emergent states" is that there are so many unknowable factors determining their development, for example the interplay of old and new forces when traditional societies break up under the pressures of modernization; the speed of economic growth in some cases and slowness in others; the pressures of reaction to the rapid and expanding urbanization and the militant growth of unemployment, especially among the increasing number of educated youth; the tensions produced by religious challenges in societies with large Muslim populations; the impact of electronically driven global capitalism on vulnerable economies; and the progress of democratization.

NOTES

1. K. Anthony Appiah, *New York Review of Books,* 24 April 1997.

2. J. Strachey, *The End of Empire* (London: Gollangz, 1952).

3. Joseph Ki-Zerbo, "Which Way Africa," in *Development Dialogue,* no. 2 (Uppsala: Hammarsskjold Foundation, 1995).

4. William Tordoff, *Government and Politics in Africa* (Bloomington: Indiana University Press, 1993).

5. Colin Legum, *Pan Africanism* (London: Pall Mall Press, 1962), and Immanual Weiss, *The Pan African Movement* (London: Methuen, 1976).

6. Harold Isaacs, *The American Negro and Africa* (Boston: Phylon, 1960).

7. Richard L. Sklar, *Post-Imperialism Concepts and Implications* (Hanover, N.H.: The Dickey Centre, Dartmouth College, 1997).

8. Legum, *Pan Africanism.*

9. René Dumont, *False Start in Africa* (London: Andre Deutsch, 1966).

10. E. J. Hobsbawm, "Ethnicity and Nationalism in Europe Today," *Anthropology Today* 8, no. 1.

11. Kenneth Christie, "The New Tribal Disorder: Ethnic Conflicts in the 1990s," in *Indicator SA* (Durban: University of Natal, 1997).

12. Adebayo Adedeji, "The Shaping of African Economics," paper delivered at the Africa at 40 conference in London, October 1997.

13. Ibid.

14. J. F. Ade-Ajayi, "Africa's Development Crisis in Perspective," in Bade, Onimode, and Synge, *Issues in African Development* (Ibadan: Heinemann, 1995).

15. Sadiq Rasheed, "Rethinking Development Strategy in Africa: The Imperative and Prospects of Human-Centered Development" (UNDP Stockholm Roundtable on Global Change, 1994).

16. For full text of the Plan of Action for Food, see Documents Section in *Africa Contemporary Record (ACR)* (New York: African Publishing, 1980–81).

17. Documents Section, *ACR* 1985–86.

18. International Monetary Fund *Survey* 26, no. 23 (15 December 1997).

19. Crawford Young, "Democracy and the Ethnic Question in Africa."

20. Richard Sklar, *Africa Insight* (Pretoria) 27, no. 1 (1997).

21. Robert B. Reich, *The Work of Nations* (New York: Vintage, 1992).

22. Peter Sutherland, *Time* (2 February 1998).

23. Ade-Ajayi, "Africa's Development Crisis in Historical Perspective."

24. Alvin Toffler, *Power-Shift* (New York: Bantam, 1990).

25. M. Scott et al., *Attitude to Africa* (London: Penguin Special, 1951).

26. UNDP Stockholm Roundtable on Global Change, 1994.

27. For a definition of a power-shift, see the previous chapter.

28. M. Castells, *The Information Age,* 3 vols. (Berkeley: University of California Press, 1998).

29. J. Lloyd, *New Statesman* (5 June 1998).

30. J. Gray, *False Dawn* (London: Granta Books, 1998).

31. G. Soros, quoted in Gray.

32. *New Statesman* (5 June 1998).

33. International Monetary Fund *Survey* 26, no. 23 (15 December 1997).

34. Ibid. 27, no. 2 (22 June 1998).

35. World Bank *Policy Research Working Paper,* WPS, 1990 (Washington, D.C.: World Bank, 1990).

36. R. McNamara, *A Global Population Policy to Advance Human Development in the 21st Century, with Particular Reference to Sub-Saharan Africa* (Kampala, Uganda: Global Coalition for Africa, 1992),

37. Cited by Jürgen Oestereich in *Courier,* journal of the European Union (Brussels), no. 31 (1998).

38. Catherine Cross, Thobias Mugadi, and Thembo Mbeki, in *Indicator SA* (Durban: University of Natal, 1998).

39. M. Leach and J. Fairhead, "Reframing Deforestation," in *Global Environmental Change* (London: Routledge, 1998).

40. SOS-Sahel, 1 Tolpuddle Street, London N1, OXT, UK.

INDEX

COLIN LEGUM now lives in Cape Town, his original home, from which he was for many years banned under apartheid. He is the author of numerous books, including *Pan-Africanism: A Brief History* and *South Africa: Crisis for the West* (with Margaret Legum). He was the founder of the *African Contemporary Record* and edited twenty-three volumes of publications. He was also co-editor of the *Middle East Survey*.